When the Nets Came Down for Brenda

By: Gene Steinmeyer

Printed by Rush Printing Co. Maryville, MO.

Prelude

Gentry Dietz was a really good basketball player. There were times, Gentry was a great basketball player. She had been a star on her Millard (Nebraska) North High School basketball team. Her twin sister, Merritt also was on that team. It was a really good team, but not a great team. Gentry's high school team came close but never won a championship of any kind.

Southern Illinois won the recruiting battle for Gentry. Merritt was a good basketball player, but she was a great track athlete. She headed to Stillwater, OK, where she would be a great star on the Oklahoma State track team.

Gentry had a good freshman season but not a great one at Southern Illinois. The Salukis weren't even a good basketball team. There certainly wouldn't be a championship for Gentry her first year away from her Omaha home. She even began to hate basketball. The thing she loved to do the most now became a job she hated.

Sometime during her sophomore season, Gentry quit basketball. She came back to Omaha convinced she would never get the chance to win that basketball championship and do the one thing she wanted to accomplish out of basketball; cut down the nets.

However, Northwest Missouri State soon came calling. I wanted Gentry to play for me. My assistant coach at that time, Lori Hopkins, started to communicate with Gentry. We brought her to the Northwest campus where I was the head women's basketball coach. We convinced her to give basketball one more attempt.

I always described the Gentry that showed up on the Northwest campus similar to a puppy in a dog pound that had been beaten with a newspaper. You raise a newspaper anywhere near that puppy and it begins shaking and whimpering, expecting another beating. Gentry was waiting to get beat up mentally again by basketball.

Gentry started to practice with our team after Christmas. She was a really good player. Sometimes, she was a great player. She had to sit out the fall semester to satisfy the NCAA residency requirements. No big deal; that only amounted to a handful of games and she could resume searching for that elusive championship; cut down that net she had only witnessed in the past.

The final pre-season practice almost became Gentry's final practice. In a drill, her knee bent in a weird angle and she heard a pop. Gentry's anterior cruciate ligament had torn. It would be another nine months before she could run full speed; nine months before she had a chance to cut down the nets with a championship team.

Gentry figured her chance at a championship was over. She quit going to classes and her grades skyrocketed downward. Mentally, she was spiraling in the wrong direction, too. Just in time, the light went on. The old, competitive Gentry was back. She barely evaded academic suspension. Maybe there would be a chance to cut down that last net after all.

Gentry was a good player her junior season. The knee held her back some of the time. She wasn't great, but she got better as the season progressed. Still no championships, but every player was scheduled to return the next season. Just as the school year began, the volleyball graduate assistant decided to give basketball a try. She stood 6 feet, 4 inches and was a really good player. She made the team more than good. We were a great team.

Gentry only had one semester of eligibility, and when she started playing in December she was good. Most of the time, she was great. Gentry was leading the team to a championship;

to a climb up a ladder for a date with a basketball net.

I really didn't know Gentry's obsession with cutting down the nets until she came into my office before the conference tournament. It was the start of March of 2011 and the beginning of a postseason run for Gentry's team.

It wasn't unusual for Gentry to come to my office. While most players thought I was just a grouchy, old coach that wasn't too approachable, Gentry plopped down often in one of my office-type chairs for a conversation about anything on her mind. The conversation this day was about winning the conference championship; cutting down the nets.

That flooded back memories of another time when another good athlete wanted to cut down nets after a championship. That athlete was Brenda Florian. Brenda was just an average sophomore basketball player on a team dominated by seniors. The seniors were good players. A couple of them were great players.

I often think about Brenda Florian, probably more than even the great players on that team. Now with Gentry hanging around my office and telling me how important it is for her to cut down nets, Brenda was the first person that hit my thoughts.

You see, Brenda never played a minute in a single game that season. However, it was Brenda on the ladder cutting the last strand of the last net at the conclusion of four different championship games. Her basketball skill isn't what made Brenda special. It was a terrible disease and the grace and courage she showed that made Brenda special.

This is the story of Brenda Florian. It is a story about 18 incredible months of courage that goes far beyond celebrating a championship. Even 30 years later, it's about celebrating one very remarkable life.

When the Nets Came Down for Brenda

Chapter 1
<u>First Memories</u>

I came to teach at Wilber-Clatonia High School the fall of 1979. It was a homecoming-type coaching move. The stars must have been lined up. It was just like it was supposed to happen.

It was the spring and I had made the 35 mile drive from Milford to attend a friend's wedding. I taught junior high math and was a boys' freshmen coach at Milford High School. I didn't have much of a function in my friend's wedding except to help serve drinks at the reception. The reception was held at the Carriage House Restaurant in Clatonia.

The Carriage House was run by the son of the owner of the Red Rooster, a famous chicken restaurant in Lincoln. My step-mother, Mae, waited tables at the Carriage House for something to keep her busy. I think Mae liked to gossip about the lousy tips some of the locals left.

I arrived in the early afternoon that sunny Friday. As I was sitting on a bench outside the post office with my dad, Billy, I saw a tall girl go into Rehm's Tavern, which was directly across the street. My dad was the postmaster at

Clatonia, and he had plenty of time to sit and talk about the world's events with his son and any local that wandered by.

I knew the Wilber-Clatonia girls' basketball team had been absolutely horrible since the female sport of basketball came to exist in Nebraska during the early 1970's. I had observed Wilber-Clatonia play in Milford during the previous school year and I don't think they hit double figures in scoring. Not just one player, but the whole team.

I asked Dad about this physical specimen walking into the local watering hole. He informed me that was the daughter of a former basketball star from Clatonia, Oren Miller. Oren's Clatonia team was the Class D state champion in 1958.

My next question was why she didn't play basketball. Dad dropped the bomb that would lead to the beginning of 33 years of head coaching. My father informed me the girl I had just seen for the first time was only an eighth grader and the whole eighth grade class was loaded with six-footers.

My uncle, Gene Else, was a former high school and college basketball coach. He warned me if I ever took the plunge into becoming a head coach, I should select a school where winning would be simple. It didn't take much imagination that Wilber-Clatonia would soon field a winner in high school girls' basketball. Now I had to find a way to become a candidate as the next coach at Wilber-Clatonia.

It just so happened that I served several drinks that night to Bob Sykes, a school board member. He told me the girls' basketball job would soon be open. My boss at Milford, Bob Bargen, had developed a state power house in boys' basketball.

That was a great starting reference. Sykes gave me the green light to go after the Wilber-Clatonia job. Paul Heller, a long-time friend and a shirt-tail relative was the principal. It was the easiest job interview I ever experienced.

The ground work was laid for what would happen four years later. My first position at Wilber-Clatonia was as the sixth grade teacher. Brenda Florian had just entered junior high. She played seventh grade basketball that year. I am ashamed to admit, I don't remember much about that seventh grade team.

My first year as a head coach was almost too easy. It marked the first year that a Wilber-Clatonia girls' team ever had a winning record. Angie Miller, Oren's daughter, was all that was advertised. She led the team in points and rebounds. The team came within one game of the state tournament.

The next year I moved a couple of doors down to become the junior high math teacher. I taught Brenda in eighth grade math and she played eighth grade basketball. My friend, Jim Moore, was the junior high coach. I have searched my memory for just the faintest hint of anything about Brenda, but nothing fires in my brain.

My second year as a head coach at Wilber-Clatonia wasn't nearly as smooth. The sophomores starred and the seniors stewed about loss of notoriety. Angie's car was vandalized and one of the seniors had made a sign in shop class. They placed it in her locker. It read, "Bitch." It was a tough year.

Brenda played freshmen basketball. However, her best sport appeared to be volleyball. That's what I was told, anyway. I still have no memory of Brenda.

I was told she was a good kid. Everyone said Brenda was a fun kid to be around. Her best friend, Lori Kreshel, was always at the Florian house. That would become very important in a couple of years. Right now, I had a big crisis just surviving my second year as a head coach.

The seniors graduated and the team started to bond. Angie was a natural leader. There was another gifted post player on the team. Her name was Penny Thompson. Together, they made a great post combination. However, the guards weren't ready for big-time games and we fell two games short of the state tournament.

It was now or never for the seniors. We would start four players that were almost six foot. That's almost unheard of in small town girls' basketball. Our point guard would be a feisty, but small and slow Chris Packer. What Chris lacked in talent she made up in guts. Her back-up, Rene Wickwire, was on the verge of becoming a pretty good point guard, too.

The school board and the superintendent thought it was do or die, also. At the beginning of the school year, my boss informed me that anything less than a state tournament appearance would mean a premature end to my head coaching career. My friend and relative, Paul Heller, was no longer the principal and my job was really in danger.

There was plenty motivation from every direction. Now I began to remember Brenda Florian. I remember she started on the volleyball team as a sophomore. I had moderate expectations for this aggressive sophomore guard in basketball. After all, we were short of guards since two senior guards had quit before the season began. I was almost sure she would make the varsity team.

Two weeks later, a week before Thanksgiving, I was wrong. Brenda Florian would not make the varsity squad just yet. It would probably happen sometime soon, but a freshman had outplayed Brenda. She would have to start the year on the junior varsity team.

That year, 1982, was when I first became aware of Brenda Florian. I am baffled as to why I have no memory of her before that fall semester. Things have a way of changing. As it would turn out, I very seldom go a single day without thinking about Brenda Florian.

Chapter 2
Losing a Father

The Florian family was packing up and moving to Wilber, NE. They had lived in Ord, NE. Doris and Jerome had built an impressive family. Alan was the first son and was 13 years old when the family moved. Then Arlene was born, followed by Brian. Brenda came into the world fourth and last but not least was Melissa, who was about one year old when she became a Wilber resident.

Brenda had swollen tonsils and the doctor said they had to come out. Doris didn't know any doctors in Wilber, so she put her faith in the Ord doctors. Dr. Markley, knowing the family had suffered some medical setbacks recently, offered to do the procedure for the exact amount the insurance was willing to pay, which was $100.

The tonsils came out and Brenda was in the pink of health as she moved into her new surroundings. At four years old, no one suspected that deadly cancer cells could already be in Brenda's body.

The move to Wilber was made by necessity. Jerome was sick; his kidneys were failing. The father found himself on disability and bound to a kidney dialysis machine. He needed the dialysis machine to stay alive and the closest one to Ord was in Grand Island. That's an hour and twenty minute drive to get to the nearest life-saving kidney machine.

Doris' parents lived in Wilber. It was a short 40 minute drive to the dialysis machine in Lincoln. It made life easier for the entire family. Doris found work and Jerome searched for odds and ends to keep busy. His sons and Brenda would mow lawns and haul people's garbage for extra spending money.

After three years on dialysis, Jerome had a kidney transplant. The procedure was a welcomed success. For the next five years, he could break the cord to the machine that had held him hostage. He hoped he had seen the last of the kidney machine.

However, there was a downside. Anti-rejection drugs were needed so Jerome's body would accept the new kidney. The powerful drugs caused severe side-effects.

Along the way, Jerome had cataracts and a spleen removed, medical issues caused by the anti-rejection medicine that allowed his new kidney to function. The drugs took their toll during those five years, and eventually Jerome had to go back on the dialysis machine. The new kidney was now failing.

Jerome's disabilities did have one very big positive affect; Jerome grew very close to his children. Brenda and Melissa especially benefited. The girls loved to have their dad read to them, which he did often. Brenda couldn't wait to ride on the riding lawn mower as the pair manicured lawns in Wilber.

The life-sustaining dialysis didn't work long this time. Sadly, Jerome's body gave out on him. He died nine years after he had moved to Wilber. Brenda was 13 years old and was devastated by her father's death. She would seek out her mom for comfort.

Often going into Doris' bedroom for security, Brenda would look for answers. She wanted to understand death. Why had death taken her dad? She peppered her mother with tough questions.

She asked questions about God. Brenda wanted to know about Heaven. She was sure her dad was in Heaven, but she wasn't sure exactly what Heaven meant. Doris assured Brenda she would meet her father in Heaven someday. No one could imagine how soon.

Melissa became very clingy to her mother. She followed her mother everywhere and hung on for dear life. She had lost a father and she wasn't about to lose her mother.

It was a pretty heavy load for a 13 year old to shoulder. Brenda had lost her beloved father, the person who would read with her, put her on his lap on the lawn mower. It was unthinkable that in a very short time, that load would become much heavier.

Chapter 3
<u>Friends for Life</u>

It probably started in third or fourth grade. Lori Kreshel wasn't exactly sure. What she was sure about the was food, the fun, and the music that made Brenda and Lori best friends. Lori spent most her time at Brenda's house. It was where best friends could have the best time. The Florian place was really cool.

Part of it could have been Brenda's older brother, Brian. Brian was the one that loved cars. He had a cool car and he was a drag racer. It was pretty neat to have a brother like that. There was the music, too. Brian and oldest brother Alan had great music. More than once did the pair of best friends get shooed out of the brothers' room or Brian's car. They could listen to great music when borrowing 8-tracks from the older brothers. _I Don't Like Spiders and Snakes_ was one of their favorites. Jim Stafford sang about insects. It's hard to believe the Branson Entertainment District regular to be cool, but in the 1970's Jim Stafford had some good music. Who could forget _Wildwood Weed_?

They were the perfect pair in school. Lori was the academic, the best in her class. Brenda was a good kid who took advantage of having a best friend who was a real brainiac. Both received good grades at Wilber Public Schools, but Brenda relied on Lori's help for her good marks.

The Kreshel house was full of kids and a loving mother. Lori describes her mom, Bonnie, as phenomenal. The trouble is her father, Ken, was an alcoholic. It made for a difficult household for Lori.

Bonnie was a very liberal mother, as Lori describes her in loving terms. She didn't care how much time Lori spent at the Florian's. Doris worked for Ken, painting houses and staining the wood work. Ken was a contractor and he built family homes. She knew why Lori liked to spend time in her house and she was happy to have Lori as a regular guest.

The coolest thing about the Florian house was the refrigerator in the bathroom. That's not exactly true. You couldn't really do your bathroom business, while grabbing a sandwich from the fridge, but it was close.

There was a pantry off the kitchen. The pantry was located by the back bedroom. There was a bathroom near the back bedroom, but it only had a sink. If you followed those directions, you get the picture of a refrigerator in a bathroom.

Your mind might picture this great kitchen appliance sitting proudly in the middle of a giant, master bathroom. However, it was close enough to the bathroom to be unique. It was cool enough that the visitors to the Florian house will never forget the fridge in the john.

Lori and Brenda were two peas in a pod. They were very seldom apart. When sleeping in a queen size bed, Brenda would stick her hand under Lori's pillow. Brenda explained it was always cool under that pillow. It seems everything about the Florian's were cool.

As the pair became teenagers, they were typical for that age; they experimented. Wilber has a culture of beer drinking. It was unusual for a teenager from Wilber not to experiment with alcohol. Lori and Brenda gave it a try. They snuck a beer now and then, but their drinking was small. It was Wilber, after all.

Mostly they just hung out. They truly liked each other. They did one other thing; the pair wrote letters to each other. They wrote all the time, about anything. As the pair grew older, they became very skilled with the written word. They didn't know it just yet, but their letter writing would someday become one of the most important things in their lives.

When the Nets Came Down for Brenda

Chapter 4
The Year of Firsts

As Brenda entered junior high, I came home to coach the girls' basketball team. I was excited and apprehensive to take the leap into being the boss of a basketball team. I knew I had a good senior class and a great freshmen class. Now I had to put together the entire structure of the team.

Steve Holmquist had just been hired at Wilber-Clatonia High School and was the new assistant volleyball coach.. We became friends almost immediately. The school had assigned Marilyn Anthony, the head volleyball coach, as my assistant.

I don't think Marilyn was real excited about the basketball job. Since Steve and I had become friends and were excited to start our coaching careers, the school let Steve replace Marilyn as my assistant. Marilyn wasn't upset and I had a close friend to assist me.

The team was ready to start a summer gym schedule and the only thing left was for me to find a student manager or two before the practices began in November. Lisa Albert came to me with a friend of hers and asked if they could be managers. I didn't know at the time, but this would be my first connection to the Florian family.

Lisa's brother is Scott Albert. I didn't know much about Scott, but I had grown up in Clatonia knowing his parents, especially his father, Skeeter. Skeeter's grandparents lived across the street from my grandparents. In 1979, Scott Albert and Arlene Florian were dating.

Arlene was the older sibling of Brenda's. Arlene was the sister Brenda could go to for those serious talks every teenager occasionally needs. Scott was two years older than Arlene and six years older than his sister, Lisa.

That first basketball season was great. The team won games, the players were terrific, and the crowds grew as the games got more important in February. It was a season of firsts. Of course, it was my first year of 33 years as a head basketball coach.

I received my first technical foul of my coaching career. It came in the conference tournament in a loss to Friend High School. Of course, I didn't deserve it; anyway that's the story I'm sticking with. The game was close and the technical may have cost the team a win. It

When the Nets Came Down for Brenda

probably taught me a lesson because I received very few technical fouls the rest of my career.

The Wilber-Clatonia girls' basketball team won their first championship ever. We defeated Humboldt High School in the district championship game. Ironically, my first teaching position had been at Humboldt. I had a talented sixth grader by the name of Paula Sue Blecha. Now, she was the star of the Humboldt team. We held her under double figures by running a special defense just for Paula Sue. The Wolverines would advance to the regional game against Hebron.

There are two distinct memories from the Humboldt triumph. After the win, the team cut down the nets. I remember I refused to go up and cut any strands, but one of the high school boys put the net around my neck for the pictures parents were taking.

The second was my first confrontation with a parent. It was a senior parent. Their daughter received limited playing time. It amazed me how we could accomplish so much and there still be sadness among the players.

There are certain firsts you never forget. My first basketball team will always live in my memories. Not all were happy. I didn't realize it at the time, but one member of that team would not be with us much longer.

Lisa, my student manager, at some point during the spring or summer of 1980 began to notice an unusual amount of bruising on her body. She kept it quiet but she must have worried. Her family thinks she knew something was wrong.

Still, Lisa kept it quiet from her friends and family. She did, however, start to do some research on her own. Her family would eventually find medical books under her mattress. Lisa was trying to figure out what was wrong.

Sometime that fall, Lisa finally gave in and asked to see a doctor. Her doctor knew immediately something was wrong. They took blood samples and did tests. Lisa's worst fears were realized; she had leukemia.

A plan was made for her recovery. First, she would go to the hospital for chemotherapy treatment. Later, there might be a bone marrow transplant. The disease was serious, but the prognosis was optimistic. Doctors were confident the leukemia could be put into remission.

That's about the time I heard about Lisa's health issues. I knew she wouldn't be my student manager for my second year of coaching, but I didn't know why. I heard about the leukemia and was happy to hear about the positive outlook for her recovery. That joy would turn to shock.

Everything was fine when Arlene went to visit Lisa on a Thursday at the hospital. Arlene lived in Lincoln and it was easy for her to stop by the hospital for a visit. On Friday, Arlene came to Wilber to be with her family. Scott and Arlene would go back to Lincoln on Sunday, stopping by to see Lisa again.

They were shocked to find Lisa clinging to life. The chemotherapy had lowered her body's resistance to infection. She had developed a canker sore in her mouth. It was just an ordinary sore that most people fight off without another thought. However, it would cost Lisa her life.

By the time Arlene got to the hospital on Sunday, Lisa was so sick they weren't letting anyone but immediate family into her hospital room. By Monday, October 19, 1980, Lisa Albert was gone. It was so quick. How could a healthy 16-year-old girl be gone so quickly?

Scott wasn't real close to his sister. There was six years difference in their age and Scott had been out of high school for two years. Then there was the boy-girl thing. All of a sudden, it was too late. Like everyone else, Scott was shocked Lisa could be gone so quickly and guilty about his distant relationship with his younger sister.

I was in shock, too. It had been my first team, my first technical, and my first team championship. However, it all seemed so small compared to my first tragedy.

Chapter 5
Pissy Missy

Melissa Florian was nine months old when the Florian family moved to Wilber. She was the youngest of the five Florian children. It's tough to remember much when you're that young. Melissa's first memories of Wilber were riding around the block on her bicycle.

Then there was her dad, Jerome. She remembers Dad being around all the time. Melissa knew he wasn't feeling well most of the time, but she really liked having him around. She would hang out with her dad while her brothers and sisters were at school. It was pretty neat having him all to herself.

After a while, Melissa found herself in school, but Dad was still there when she got home. He would read to Brenda and her. She could steal more time with her father than her older brothers and sisters. That was pretty neat.

Melissa wanted to hang out with Brenda, too. Brenda was about four years older. That was a problem; Brenda didn't want to spend much time with her little sister. Melissa was a pest. She wanted to know everything, every detail.

Lori and Brenda were always together. Melissa wanted to make it a three member gang. The older girls were mean to her. They ignored the younger girl. They denied her what she wanted the most, information. Melissa was a sponge. She had to know it all.

Brenda and Melissa fought like crazy. Doris said her daughters clawed each other until they bled. Melissa could proudly claim the scars on Brenda's hands were inflicted by her. Still, Melissa wanted to be part of the older group. She could take the punishment and dish it out, too.

Brenda and Lori talked about a lot of things that younger girls wanted to know. Melissa especially wanted to know about the boys in the older girl's lives. She would eavesdrop on the pair. She couldn't wait to hear what boy her sister thought was hot. Even Melissa said she was a pest. She just didn't want to miss out on anything. Melissa definitely earned her nickname, "Pissy Missy."

After her dad died, Melissa was afraid something would happen to her mother. She didn't want to lose sight of her mom. She followed Doris everywhere. Just about the time things were returning to normal, Brenda got sick.

Melissa was probably too young to understand the exact seriousness of the disease that had attacked her sister's body. Brenda lost her leg, but now she was going to get better. That's what they told her.

Brenda seemed to be getting sicker, but then a neat thing happened. Some people were giving Brenda, Melissa and her mother a trip to Disney World. Melissa couldn't wait to see Mickey Mouse and all his friends. She couldn't wait for her first plane ride.

That was one neat trip. Mickey Mouse came right to their hotel room to visit with Brenda and Melissa. Melissa wanted to do everything and see everything. However, the sister that Melissa had trouble keeping up with wasn't feeling well.

Still, Melissa hated when they had to leave early. Brenda needed the comfort of home. She also needed Pissy Missy right by her side.

When the Nets Came Down for Brenda

Chapter 6
The Gang from the
<u>Old School Yard</u>

I personally was in for major changes during my sophomore year of high school. The school districts of Wilber and Clatonia combined during the 1965-1966 school year. I had spent the first ten years of school at Clatonia. The school itself was an old brick building set at the far west end of Clatonia on Highway 42. A gymnasium made of cement block was attached to the north side of the building.

Clatonia only had 220 people in 1965. The old, brick school was two stories high. The gym was just short of regulation size. There were only three or four rows of seats, but people could huddle on the stage or sit on folding chairs that were against the wall on the south end. The surface was made of tile. If it was humid outside, it was as slick as a skating rink inside. No one seemed to mind.

One time as a kid, I was drinking a pop in a glass bottle during a Clatonia basketball game. I was stationed on one of those folding chairs. A high school player dove for a loose ball and hit me square in the pop bottle, which hit me square on a front tooth. It chipped the tooth and I proudly displayed that indentation to my smile for years to come.

The playground was covered in gravel. It wasn't exactly as soft as today's playgrounds. The gravel wasn't as near as soft as the shredded rubber you find on today's playgrounds. The jungle gym was a complex of squares and triangles. At least once a year, someone fell off and required a few stitches. No one thought of blaming the equipment.

My favorite was the teeter-totter. I loved to try and balance with my partner, seeing how long we could go without our feet or the board touching the ground. We also played "bucking bronco" on the teeter-totter. I would slam my end hard to the ground, trying to throw my friend on the other end to the ground.

My first impression of my new school at Wilber was how similar it was to Clatonia School. Located in the middle of Wilber, it was an old, brick building. It was, however, one story higher than the Clatonia structure. The gym surface was an improvement over the tile floor in Clatonia. It had a soft wood floor but there were a couple of problems.

First, it also was used as the stage where school plays, musicals, and convocations were held. That made the playing surface slick. The floor was very small. It didn't have a distinct half court line.   If you tried too hard for a loose ball on the east sideline, you would fall off a four-foot stage. That would cause you to tumble onto the score table or an unforgiving cement floor.

The playground was pretty similar, too. It had the normal playground equipment, although the jungle gym didn't seem quite so dangerous. In 1970, the school district built a brand, new high school and the old high school building and playground were used exclusively for the elementary grades.

The elementary school playground is where Brenda and her gang hung out and played.   Most of their spare time was spent at the playground. Brenda's gang was girls from the neighborhood. The two shortest in height were Chris Packer and Renee Wickwire. When they got to high school, the pair would compete against each other for playing time at point guard. The mortician's daughter was part of the group, too. Ginger Zajicek was a year older but a permanent member of the pack of females at the Elementary School playground.

All four were athletic, some more than others. Brenda and Ginger were natural athletes. Chris and Renee were just tough. What those two lacked in athleticism, they made up in having nasty attitudes. If you wanted a pair of friends to always have your back, Chris and Renee were that pair.

Chris' first image when thinking back to the playground was the sandburs. The area was sparsely covered with grass, gravel, rocks and weeds. The problem was the weeds dominated. You couldn't do much without picking off the annoying burrs from you socks.

Brenda was a regular to the playground, but she would come and go as her family needed her. Jerome, Brenda's father, was sick and the family was always doing odd jobs to raise a little extra money.

Brenda would call a time-out to do a paper route or mow a neighbor's lawn. Doris, Brenda's mother explained the need for the extra money. "They would use the money for school lunches or for an ice cream cone." To Chris, the Florian family was always on the move.

Now in high school, the Elementary School Yard Gang all knew the 1982-1983 season would be special. The first memory for Chris that fall came while standing in the lunch line as the basketball season neared. Brenda and Chris were talking. The subject was on Brenda's sore right knee. "The knee had just started to give her problems," Chris said. "I remember she was worried people would think she was a 'wuss'.

We thought it was cartilage if there was something wrong."

The gang always worried about each other; they played, they fought and they competed, but they always cared. The group that picks sandburs together sticks together.

When the Nets Came Down for Brenda

Chapter 7
Decision and Discover

It's easy to get ahead of myself when talking about Brenda. This isn't a cliff hanger where Brenda gets sick and the magic of medicine saves her life. This isn't a story of miracles and cliff hangers. It's a story of one person's courage, a family's tragedies, and how 30 years later, the story stays fresh in the minds of every character.

Somewhere, Brenda has to transform from a normal, 16-year-old teenager to this hero of courage and faith. It started for me in the fall of 1982. Brenda had caught my attention by becoming a sophomore starter on the volleyball team. Steve Holmquist began as my basketball assistant coach, but his real interest was in volleyball. Marilyn Anthony gave up the coaching reins to the volleyball team and Steve took over. Steve, a good friend and good basketball coach, left the basketball team to concentrate on his own team.

Dave Grothen, the high school mathematics teacher, moved into the assistant coaching position and Jim Moore moved up from the junior high basketball team to become my freshmen coach. Both were good guys, friends of mine, and anxious to help the girls' basketball team reach its full potential.

It was a rocky start to the season. Sherry Kreshel, Lori's older sister, and Jill Fritz, both seniors chose not to play. Neither were great talents, but they had both played significant minutes their junior years. Neither was crucial to the team's success, but Sherry's father, Ken, was on the school board and Jill's mother was an outspoken critic of my choice of players for significant playing time.

The real reason I wasn't overly concerned was I had a group of young, enthusiastic, and talented guards who were ready and able to take the older players' places. Jalylene Sandgren, Deb Keller, Ina Rochelle, Rene Wickwire, and a feisty starter from the volleyball team, Brenda Florian, were more than capable of carrying the load on this talented team.

Practice began in the middle of November. Angie Miller and Penny Thompson, the star post players were tearing up the gym. Seniors Beccy Duba and Robin Broz looked like they had new-found confidence. Chris Packer took charge at point guard. There weren't many surprises as the team got ready for their season opener the first of December. The one surprise none of the coaches could quite figure out was the poor play of Brenda Florian.

Dave had coached Brenda as a freshman on the junior varsity team. The one thing he could always count on was the break-neck play of Brenda. What she lacked in talent, she made up in hustle and toughness. Now as a sophomore competing for a varsity position, Brenda wasn't the same.

Dave, Jim and I talked about it. Dave wondered if Brenda was "dogging" it. He noted she just couldn't get up and down the floor. Brenda was on the bubble to making the varsity team and it appeared she wasn't giving it her best effort.

"In hindsight," Dave recalled, "Brenda complained to me about her knee. I thought, oh man, we got a girl that isn't really trying and making excuses by making up pain." That thought has bothered Dave even 30 years later.

But Dave wasn't the only one that noticed Brenda's apparent lack of hustle. Jim and I had also seen the change in Brenda's play. The three of us discussed it and Brenda came out 13th on a 12-player roster. Most people think the toughest decision a coach makes is deciding a starting line-up. In truth, I've agonized more over the years making decisions on the back end of the team. That was the case with Brenda.

After Thanksgiving, I had to announce my decision. Our first game was less than two weeks away and varsity uniforms had to be handed out. I felt Brenda needed to be told in private and not by just putting a list on a bulletin board.

The moment of that discussion is my first real memory of Brenda Florian. There would be many more to significant times ahead. I called Brenda into the room that doubled as a weight room and a training room. Wilber-Clatonia didn't have much of a weight room. There was a universal set of weights and a few free weights, but it was a sad collection compared to today's training facilities.

Brenda plopped up on the training table. In my three-plus years at Wilber-Clatonia, I had taped hundreds of ankles on that table. The room was completely empty except for Brenda, Dave and me. I got right to the point and let Brenda know she hadn't made the varsity team.

I tempered it by telling Brenda, with a little more effort, she could easily pass one of the younger players in a short period of time. I'll never forget what she told me. "You're right, coach. I just haven't had my heart in it," Brenda said. She promised that would change.

It was then she told me about how badly her knee hurt. "During volleyball, it felt like it was tearing inside when I dove on the floor," she said. Brenda told me the knee hadn't gotten any better and she wanted me to look at it.

I wasn't much of an athletic trainer, but I was the best on staff at Wilber-Clatonia. I knew my weakness. However, I had an ace-in-the-hole at the Crete Hospital. Chuck Bolton was a physical therapist in Crete, 10 miles to the north of Wilber. I promised Brenda I would call him and set up a visit.

Chuck would look at the injury like an athletic trainer. I was confident he would diagnose and suggest the right treatment. The appointment was set for the first Tuesday in December, less than one week from the start of the season.

That began an 18-month odyssey for the Wilber teenager. It would leave a mark on many lives and have a huge effect on our basketball team. The story of strength, courage, and faith was about to begin.

When the Nets Came Down for Brenda

Chapter 8
<u>The Odyssey Begins</u>

Brenda went to see Chuck Bolton at the Crete Hospital. I knew Chuck, not as the physical therapist, but as the head athletic trainer at Kearney State College (now the University of Nebraska-Kearney). I knew Chuck would look at Brenda's knee and recommend treatment that would get her back on the court as soon as possible.

Chuck had been good to me. He had examined my young step-daughter, Stephanie Vogt, when she was diagnosed with Asgood-Schlatter, a painful lump just below the knee. The first doctor that discovered the Asgood-Schlatter had told us to get an immobilizer and stop all activity. Keeping Stephanie inactive wasn't much of an option.

We went to Chuck for a second opinion. He told us that was an outdated treatment for Asgood-Schlatter. The best thing Stephanie could do is continue with sports until the pain became unbearable. At that point, ice the knee. Eventually, it would cure itself. That's exactly what we did and it worked like a charm.

However, my first encounter with Chuck had nothing to do with knees or daughters. It involved fear. As a sophomore at Kearney State College, I was cruising with a grade of an "A" in Anatomy class. About halfway through the semester, the professor died of a sudden coronary. Chuck was chosen to take over the class. By the time the final exam had been completed, my grade had plummeted to a "C" and I was lucky to get it.

The next semester, I took his Kinesiology class. Familiarity did not lead to better grades. His final test involved recognizing and naming every muscle in the body. I was ecstatic to be awarded another "C" for a final grade.

Chuck was very thorough and very intelligent. Despite my very average grades, I knew he wouldn't let me down with Brenda. However, even a man of his skills couldn't get Brenda back on the basketball floor. He knew the problem wasn't muscular. Brenda needed X-rays and a specialist.

Dr. Robert Travnicek was Brenda's family doctor in Wilber. With a reference from Chuck, "Trav," as we called the great family doctor, took X-rays of the right knee.

Trav was known for his bluntness. He didn't mince words or shy away from a little pain for his patients. Arlene and Brian, Brenda's older siblings, knew that fact first hand. "He would scare the crap out of you," Arlene said.

Brian had personal proof of that. He had a red spot and asked Trav to get rid of it. "He gave me a shot on the red spot and got out his soldering iron. Then he grabbed my hair and yelled, "Don't move!"

Trav was tough but he was great about finding specialist for special problems. An immediate appointment was scheduled with a doctor in Lincoln. No one had made a diagnosis or even made a prediction, but something wasn't right.

Trav was sure about one thing and he called Doris with the second sports disappointment of the week for Brenda. "There won't be any basketball this season." Trav told Brenda's mother, Doris.

The next day, Brenda was in Lincoln. After an exam by the specialist and an evaluation of the X-rays, the doctor had more bad news. There was something growing in the knee that shouldn't be there. He scheduled an immediate visit at the famous Mayo Clinic in Rochester, MN.

Thursday morning, Doris, Arlene and Brenda began their first of many trips to Minnesota. They arrived in Rochester late Thursday afternoon. Brenda had a Friday appointment with the doctors. No one knew the sudden and immediate changes that lay just days ahead.

When the Nets Came Down for Brenda

Chapter 9
<u>The Final Jog</u>

Rochester, MN had about 100,000 residents in 1982. That didn't seem very big for having such a world-famous hospital. Anyone who wanted the best treatment to a variety of diseases headed for this Minnesota city. Rochester was situated less than 100 miles southeast of Minneapolis.

It only took a day for Brenda to obtain an appointment at the Mayo Clinic. The doctors in Nebraska sped up the process and Brenda, her mother and sister were waiting for their first meeting with the Mayo doctors by mid-morning on the first Friday of December, 1982.

Brenda had several appointments set for that morning. The trio walked into the first waiting room and found it filled with people. They prepared for a long wait, but once Brenda gave her name to the receptionist, she was put to the top of the list.

"Everywhere we went, they knew we were coming," Arlene said. "We wouldn't even sit down and they would usher us right in."

"That was alarming right away. It sent chills through me. It was scary right away. It sent flags up."

By early afternoon, Brenda was given some ominous news by the Mayo doctors. They told her they now knew what was growing on her thigh bone just above her right knee. It was called Osteogenic Sarcoma. It was cancer and it was attached to the bone.

If they could stop it right now, Brenda would live. The cancer traveled by the bone marrow. The first stop for the cancerous cells would be the lungs. However, the doctors thought they had caught it early enough. But the only way to stop it from traveling up the bone marrow was to cut it out. It meant amputation of Brenda's right leg above where the cancer was growing.

Surgery was scheduled for Monday. Brenda had less than 72 hours before her life would change dramatically forever. She knew her athletic career was probably over. No volleyball, no basketball, no jogging the streets of Wilber. Even though the knee hurt, there was time for one final jog. Arlene jogged regularly. However, she had only jogged with Brenda a few times. Now Brenda asked Arlene to go with her for one final time.

Doris had the horrible experience of losing her husband after a long illness. It was unthinkable that her 16 year old daughter could have her life in danger, too. It was a very emotional time for Doris. The jog helped Doris by blocking reality, if only for a short time.

"Mom was upset and more emotional than Brenda or me," Arlene said. "It was good for Brenda to step away." It would not be the last time Brenda would do things to protect her mother.

Brenda realized this would be the final activity she would do with two legs. The girls got ready for a run. Doris wouldn't let her daughter too far from her sight. She demanded to follow the pair in the car. She just couldn't stand the thought of Brenda breaking down on the jog. She wouldn't let the jog turn into another crisis.

By standards of most joggers, the run didn't last long. "I think it hurt her so much that we didn't get far," Arlene said. "I think we got a mile in or something like that." However, that was a great accomplishment for someone with a tumor growing on her thigh bone.

After the jog, it was an agonizing wait until the surgery on Monday. Arlene was determined not to have her sister sit in the hotel room and stress over the coming events.

There was a Cracker Barrel Restaurant in Rochester and Saturday the three Florians dined there. Arlene remembered the peanuts they ate at the Cracker Barrel. The older sister dragged the family on a shopping trip. Arlene would try anything to distract Brenda from the surgery on Monday.

Besides eating and shopping, Brenda spent a big chunk of the weekend calling family and friends. "Her attitude didn't have much to do with the life and death struggles associated with cancer," Arlene said. "That aspect of her death didn't seem real. The main topic on the phone that weekend was losing her leg."

"The big topic was no more sports. She asked questions like, "What will I do?" or "Can I have a family?" or "Can I clean my house." I told her that's what you have other people do for you. I tried to quell her fears."

Despite all the worries, Brenda was confident that the cancer would be gone when the right leg was amputated. Life would continue.

Chapter 10
Surgery, Recovery, Normalcy

Brenda is in trouble, much more trouble than Brian first thought. Brenda's older brother had just graduated from Milford Technical College in auto body. His first full-time job was in York, NE, about an hour's drive from Wilber. Brian was coming back to Wilber for the weekend, to have fun with friends. Now all his thoughts were on his younger sister.

Brian had heard the news from Rochester. When Brenda first experienced pain in the knee, people thought it was muscular. Later, when a lump appeared, they thought it might be a water build-up. However, Brenda had cancer growing on her leg bone. The only way to get rid of the cancer was to cut off the leg. That was the hard truth that occupied Brian's thoughts on the drive to Wilber.

Brian looked at his right leg that was pressing on the accelerator. How will it be for Brenda without her right leg? How could his little sister ever get back to normal? "It freaks you out what she is going through," Brian said. "If it were me, what would it be like?" Tough questions the young adult struggled to answer.

The weekend was tough for Brenda, Arlene and Doris. Now it was time for the surgery.   Once again, events began to happen quickly. The surgeons who had removed the leg above the knee had also pulled skin over the stump of the leg. That part of the surgery would heal pretty quickly.

It seemed like she had barely got her senses back when the doctors had Brenda on the move. They had Brenda go to counseling. Doris explained the goal of seeing a counselor. "They wanted to make her mind know her leg wasn't there." That would be an issue for the next 18 months.

After the leg had been removed, the doctors had cast over what remained of the right leg. They did this to provide weight to the right side of Brenda's body, giving her balance. With this balance, the physical therapist almost immediately began working with Brenda on handling her crutches.

She caught on quickly. Brenda was getting more mobile and the counselors were satisfied with her state of mind. All that was left for Brenda was to go home to Wilber and try to become a normal teenager again. However, Brenda was far from normal and it had little to do with her loss of a leg.

Before the trio left Minnesota, they had a talk with the doctors about Brenda's prognosis. They told the Florian's that they thought the surgery had gotten all of the cancer. Brenda would have to come back for monthly scans, but no radiation or chemotherapy was scheduled. It might have been intentional positive information.

Thinking back, Doris suspects the reason for the doctor's optimism for a full recovery. "After they amputated her leg, I think they saw that. I got the drift from the doctors and nurses; they didn't want to ruin our Christmas."

Arlene agrees with her mother. "I think we had false hopes. Maybe that's what you have to do; I kind-of think you have to lay it all out there. Then we went back to Rochester and we thought it was all taken care of and she'll be just fine."

The talk on the way home was of what good came from the diagnosis and surgery. "Honestly, a naïve teenager doesn't think anything bad will happen to them. I don't think you realize what cancer really can do," Arlene said.

"I told her you're really lucky. You don't have a leg, but you have everything else. You don't have to do chemo and you don't have to do radiation." Brenda wasn't sure what that type of treatment involved. "That was news to her that she didn't have to do all that," Arlene said.

Once back home in Wilber, it didn't take long for Brenda to find the normalcy of school and friends. She almost immediately went back to school, even if only a couple of hours a day. It wasn't long before Brenda was going to school all day long.

"Brenda didn't want the kids to think she was different," Doris said. Getting back to school was the first hurdle. Now, she might even get to sit the bench for a basketball game. That would really prove she was back to normal.

Best Friends

Lori

Brenda

The Florian Family

The Florian Family, taken about 1976 – Back Row: Brenda, Arlene, Brian, Alan;
Front Row: Melissa, Doris and Jerome, who passed away in 1978.

The nets came down after one of the four championships.

Brenda was always protective of her mother Doris.

Chapter 11
Back With the Team

    While Brenda worked very hard to adapt to the challenges of living with one leg, the basketball season began. Their fallen teammate was never far from any of the basketball players' and coaches' minds. Brenda was providing motivation, even without her presence.

    The season opened the first Friday in December with a 56 – 18 thumping of conference rival Southern. Diller provided an interesting challenge by throwing strange defenses at the two 6-0 Wilber-Clatonia stars, Angie Miller and Penny Thompson.

    One of the Elementary School Gang came to the rescue. Ginger Zajicek became the first player other than Angie and Penny to score in double figures in the 41 – 24 win over Diller.

    In Rochester, Brenda was working much harder than any player or coach with one goal in mind; to come back to Wilber and return to school and all her friends and teammates.

    After Monday's surgery, Brenda had progressed so much on the crutches that the doctors gave her an out-patient pass. Brenda, accompanied by her mom and sister, headed for the mall to Christmas shop.

Brenda was ready for serious Christmas shopping. Using the pass on Saturday and Sunday, Brenda proudly proclaimed in a newspaper article, "I got all my shopping done and really enjoyed the day with Mom and Arlene."

On December 14, 1982, Brenda was released from the Mayo Clinic. It was a grueling trip back to Nebraska, but Brenda slept most of the way. When she arrived home, she found a surprise her 12-year-old sister had created. Melissa had made a sign she put on the front of the family house. It read, "Welcome Home, B.F."

The team heard Brenda was on her way home when they faced defending Class D State champion, Adams. Wilber-Clatonia had never defeated the Hornets, but a little inspiration from a fallen teammate paid off. In the end, the Wolverines ran away with a 59 – 37 win.

There was healing that needed to take place as Brenda waited for the prosthesis to be fitted for her right leg. The stump, cast for balance, had to heal. Brenda also had to wait for the swelling in the stump to retreat.

Brenda, with the stump, cast and all, began coming to practices and games. She started sitting at the end of the Wolverine bench, keeping stats and encouraging her teammates. The team responded with a 30-point win over another conference school, Tecumseh. As Christmas break arrived, Brenda was getting close to her first prosthesis.

Lori Kreshel was at her best friend's side immediately. She explained the steps Brenda had to take to be able to wear a new right leg. "Her prosthesis came in parts. At first, they had to let her stump heal so she just had to be with her stump. Then there was a weird piece that went on the end of her stump. It had a big screw and the fake leg screwed on the bottom of that. It was very rudimentary."

"The memories of her new leg are many," Lori said, "like putting powder in the little sock, poking her stump into the leg, strapping the harness on. I was so sad a 17-year-old had to deal with that."

Meanwhile, the basketball season rolled along. It was difficult for the basketball players to see what Brenda had to endure. However, she demanded no tears from her teammates. She was back with the team and she expected the team to play harder since she couldn't.

The team didn't let her down. They roared into the Christmas break beating arch-rival Tri-County 55 – 42. The Wolverines dominated the Bradshaw Christmas Tournament. Angie scored

40 points for the first time in her career against East Butler in the championship game.

Brenda could concentrate on school, motivating a basketball team and healing. She certainly didn't have to worry about Christmas shopping.

Chapter 12
<u>The Price of Inspiration</u>

There was absolutely no question Brenda was having a great effect on the Wilber-Clatonia girls' basketball team. The team was undefeated and unchallenged as Christmas came and went. The team had a lot of talent, but talent doesn't always make a great team.

What wasn't present on that team were the little things that hold back good teams from greatness. Brenda's illness wasn't a little thing. If you compare normal jealousy and petty differences found on most teams, Brenda's cancer made all those problems seem so small.

This was my fourth year at Wilber-Clatonia Schools. I couldn't believe the change in my team. There had been so many obstacles that got in the way of the team's success during those first three years. One mother, in a letter, accused me of playing only the players that partied and drank alcohol. Since her daughter didn't drink, she didn't get to play much.

I knew my players weren't angels in their personal lives, but I was pretty sure I didn't keep score on their alcohol consumption. I had another parent jump me in person after the third season. He informed me his daughter could average 20 points a game like Angie and Penny if I let her shoot as much. I tried to think back to the speech where I restricted my player's shooting.

It was true the administration had added pressure on my head for post season success, but that seemed a distant memory now that we had begun our journey with Brenda as our inspiration. A lot of credit went to the high school principal, Ernie Talerico. Ernie's support deflected much of the pressure.

None of this would have been possible if Brenda had just disappeared from the school scene. She had every right to do just that. Life had given the teenager a tough break when her father died so young. Many young people would have just given up when cancer added more suffering for Brenda.

Brenda fought back, but it came with a price. I have heard that when someone loses a limb, often phantom pains come with the recovery. That was true for Brenda. Lori knew her friend was having problems. "She struggled with phantom pains a lot, just that feeling you had to scratch your leg but it wasn't there."

Brenda's mother experienced first-hand it was much worse than an itch. "When she wore her prosthesis, it wasn't bad," Doris said.

"When she didn't have it on, she had a lot of pain."

"One night she was moaning and groaning and was very restless. I got in bed with her. I was rubbing her leg she didn't have. Then she settled down and went to sleep. She got up in the morning and asked, "Mom, were you rubbing my leg last night? I thought you were and it really felt good."

The prosthesis helped with the phantom pains and it helped with her balance. However, since the amputation was above the knee, mobility was more of an issue. "She didn't like wearing the leg because she felt like she didn't walk straight," her mother said. "She did very good with it."

Brenda had a good sense of humor when her equilibrium failed her. Her sister, Arlene, became a victim of that humor when Brenda would fall. "She would trip in the hallway and blame me for tripping her."

Her best friend also was a target. "She would fall and blame me," Lori said. "She would say I can't believe you pushed me."
When most people would feel sorry for themselves, Brenda would always find something to smile about. Looking at her prosthesis Brenda commented to her best

friend, "I guess I have one less leg to shave. That was her spirit. It was just like, oh well."

Brenda used her new handicap to break the ice with adults that had trouble dealing with a 16 year old that was fighting for her life. Dave Grothen, the assistant basketball coach and mathematics teacher, was one of those adults. "I'm not real good with those situations," Dave admitted.

The amazing high school sophomore made sure her assistant coach would be comfortable talking to her. "I still have memories of Brenda coming into my room after her leg had been removed. She just sat on my desk and there was the stump."

Lori recalled the same incident, but with a different twist. Her memory of that confrontation had Brenda sitting on the desk and taking off her prosthesis as a way of shocking Dave into conversation.

Brian, Brenda's older brother, had a 1976 Camaro sitting in the family garage. Many people thought the loss of her right leg had cost her the ability to drive. That is tough on a 16 year old who has been dreaming of driving since she could see over the dash board.

Brian did not have that opinion. "After she lost her leg, she was worried about driving. I said, "Bull crap, you can drive." I told her to get in the car and let's go. I taught her to get that leg (the stump) out of the way and flip the other one over. It was an automatic and I told her she could drive with the left foot just like your right foot."

"She wanted to drive really bad. She would call it pound the pavement. We'd go up and down. I bet we used a half a tank of gas."

Brenda wasn't satisfied with just driving a car with an automatic transmission. She wanted to drive a stick shift. That posed a problem. You needed two feet working the clutch, the break and the accelerator. Lori found the solution.

"Brenda had some wishes and we did the wishes," Lori said. "One was she wanted to drive a stick shift car. I had a stick shift. She got in my car and she threw her prosthesis over my left leg. My left leg went under hers and I did the gas. We drove around Wilber with a stick shift. She killed it a million times."

The basketball team witnessed all this courage. Little annoyances were thrown off the team. Brenda kept inspiring and the team rolled to a 9 – 0 record. We were ranked number one in the state as we prepared for our biggest challenge of the season. The team boarded the bus in early January and headed to Utica to face an undefeated Centennial team.

When the Nets Came Down for Brenda

Chapter 13
The Intimidator

Centennial was a conference school. The girls' basketball team was young but loaded with talent. Wilber-Clatonia had two 6-0 seniors and Centennial countered with two 6-0 sophomores.

Angie Miller and Penny Thompson, the Wolverines two post players had led the team in almost every offensive category. Penny had proved to be every bit as dangerous of an offensive weapon as Angie, but Angie had gotten more early recognition. Penny led the team in rebounding. As a sophomore, Penny had set a team record of 23 rebounds at Dorchester.

However, this was Angie's team. She was the undisputed leader. Angie had earned that right with her hard work and the tough times she had faced when older players resented her leadership abilities. Angie also could be intimidating.

Brenda was now a regular at practices and games. That really impressed Angie. "Here's a kid two years younger and she may not make it," Angie said. "Yet she's acting normal. She may die, but she's laughing and joking around."

Brenda also was on the bus that headed to Utica that night. She wasn't going to miss the game that promised to define much of the season.

The two teams lived up to their expectations. The post players on both sides dominated the scoring, but Wilber-Clatonia took the early lead. However, Centennial would not let the Wolverines pull away as they had done to other opponents all season.

As the clock wound down, the Centennial post players seemed to score on every possession. However, they were forced to foul to stop the clock. Angie and Penny combined to make 10 consecutive free throws in the last two minutes of the game. Finally, Wilber-Clatonia made a crucial stop in the last 20 seconds and came away with a 50 – 45 hard earned win.

A happy Brenda and team boarded the bus for the hour drive back to the Wilber-Clatonia High School. Thinking about Brenda and the struggles she would face, Brenda continued to amaze the most intimidating player on the team. "I remember the bus ride home," Angie said. "She was sitting with Ginger (Zajicek). They were laughing and having a good time. I thought, I couldn't be that strong."

After a 60-point road win over Dorchester, the team returned home for a game with

Milford. The news of Angie's skills had gotten to college campuses. On this night, recruiters from the University of Nebraska, South Florida, Doane College, and Midland College were in the stands.

The game would be a blow-out from the start, but it didn't go real smooth for Angie. She got in early foul trouble. When she came back, the team already had the game well in hand, so it wasn't long until she was back on the bench with Brenda, while the reserves finished the game.

It didn't matter to the college coaches. South Florida offered Angie a college visit that night. A trip to Tampa in the middle of a Nebraska winter sounded pretty good. However, Angie was a girl that didn't like to get too far from home, so she eventually declined the visit.

Friend High School was no match for the Wolverines, falling by 35 points and class D Lewiston held their own for a while with a tough man to man defense, but Wilber-Clatonia pulled away in the second half, winning the game 47 – 23. Ironically, twice during the season, the Wolverines were held under 50 points. Both times the teams were smaller Class D teams.

By now, it was the first week of February and time for the conference tournament. We would have to win two games against our half of the conference on Tuesday and Thursday. If we won both of those, we would face the winner of the other half of the conference. All the games would be played in Utica, the home court of our closest rival, Centennial.

It would be a grueling week, even for the healthiest student. It didn't matter to Brenda. There was too much on the line not to be on the bench for every minute of basketball action.

Wilber-Clatonia dismantled Milford again on Tuesday. That set up a rematch with the host school on Thursday. Centennial made another good run at the Wolverines, but the state's number one team prevailed 61 – 58. A win on Saturday would make it a clean sweep of conference titles since they had already wrapped up the regular season championship.

Henderson had won the other half, but Wilber-Clatonia couldn't be denied. Making their fourth trip of the year to the Centennial gym, the Wolverines treated it like their own. Nothing could deny the team their first major championship of the year.

Henderson did all they could to stop Angie. That allowed Penny to take advantage. She scored a career high. By the time Renee Wickwire hit a scoop shot at the halftime buzzer, the game was out of hand. It was never close after that circus shot.

Then it happened for the first time. Tradition says the winning team cuts down the nets. All the players took their turn cutting the cords off the rim. Finally, there was just one net left and one squad member left. She hadn't played a second of any of the games. As a matter of fact, she hadn't even put on a uniform.

It didn't matter. Brenda, with the help of her teammates, climbed up the ladder to cut down those final strands. "I don't remember ever talking about it," Angie said. "It was just what she was going to do. It felt like it was an unwritten rule. We were bound and determined that Brenda was going to cut down the nets."

I don't know if it started right at that moment or if Angie felt this way since Brenda returned from the Mayo Clinic. Whatever the timetable, the team leader who led her team with an iron will and demanding attitude was daunted by the seriously ill sophomore.

"I was intimidated by Brenda because she was so strong," Angie said. "If it had been me, I would be feeling sorry for myself." The team would be tough to beat with two strong leaders and an immeasurable amount of inspiration.

When the Nets Came Down for Brenda

Chapter 14
<u>Hug Me, Hug Me</u>

As the team sat on top of the conference and Brenda had cut down her first net, not all the news was great. Brenda had gone back to Mayo in January. The high hopes of getting all the cancer with the amputation of Brenda's right leg were squashed. The cancer, called seeds, had appeared on Brenda's lungs.

Since that discovery, Brenda carried a heavy load with the reality of this type of cancer. "The doctors told Brenda that if the seeds showed up on her lungs she would have a year to live," Lori said. "They started removing the seeds. They maimed her breasts by removing them. She just looked terrible. That was a real sacrificial thing to give up."

Brenda had endured her first of four lung surgeries. The appearance of the seeds was horrible, but I personally didn't understand the terrible reality. I don't think many players on the team knew the seriousness of the discovery of the seeds. It certainly didn't slow down Brenda.

However, she knew that chemotherapy was now necessary. The affects would be devastating to most teenagers. Brenda faced the loss of her hair and her eyelashes. It would be tough to endure, but Brenda faced it with the same positive attitude that had helped her rebound from the amputation.

Ginger Zajicek, one of her friends from the Elementary School Playground, struggled with Brenda's disease from the beginning. "It happened so quickly," Ginger said. "I remember after hearing thinking that it's not true. It couldn't happen. I think it was difficult to play after I heard that, but I was doing it for Brenda."

Two 20-point wins over Pius X and Exeter after the conference championship helped avenge two difficult losses the previous season. Pius X had won a controversial game in overtime and Exeter had ended the Wilber-Clatonia season in the district tournament. The Wolverines roared into the post-season with a 53 – 27 win over Hebron. It was their 20th win of the season.

Wilber-Clatonia had the same starting line-up for every one of the 20 games. Angie Miller, Penny Thompson, Robin Broz, Beccy Duba, and Chris Packer had been the five to gather around the jump circle for the opening tip each time.

Ginger was the first player off the bench in every game. She was quick and had a great jump shot. Ginger had become a real threat to score. She probably played more minutes than some of the starters, but she never complained about her position on the undefeated team.

In an early game, Ginger's scoring was crucial in a win. After the game, one of the players yelled at Ginger that she should have passed her the ball instead of shooting so much. Angie Miller quickly jumped in and stopped the confrontation.

"She told me to keep shooting," Ginger recalled. "We had a strong leader in Angie but our motivation was Brenda. We all knew how bad Brenda wanted to play. We wanted to do something for her."

The result was Ginger and her teammates sold bumper stickers, with the money earned going to Brenda. The bumper stickers read, "Brenda and the Wolverines – They Never Give Up." I'm pretty sure we didn't raise much money, but it gave the whole team a chance to show Brenda how much she meant to us.

The district tournament didn't provide much resistance for the Wolverines. They defeated Friend by 45 points in the opening round. The team followed it up with a 61 – 16 thumping of Pawnee City. In the championship game, Wilber-Clatonia would face Palmyra.

Leah Carsten was another one of those valuable reserves. She had a dry sense of humor that often broke up the team with her wise cracks. Her sister had been a senior when the current seniors were sophomores. Leah was aware of the conflicts on that previous team. It wouldn't happen with this team. Leah was the perfect teammate in a team dominated by seniors.

She played a lot of minutes in the three district games at Sterling High School. Palmyra players were big and strong, but didn't provide much competition. Wilber-Clatonia scored at will through most of the game, winning by a score of 76 – 42. Despite the recent bad news and lung surgery, Brenda was in her normal place on the bench.

She joined her teammates in celebrating the district title. Leah remembers Brenda from that jubilation. "We were all on the floor and Brenda came on the floor," Leah said. "We were all hugging. I gave her a big hug. She was sore from her recent surgery and she winced. I said I was sorry, but Brenda said, "Hug me, hug me!"

Not only did Leah and everyone else hug Brenda, but they boosted her up the ladder for a second time. Despite the easy wins, the nets were coming down and Brenda cut the last strands of the last net. It wouldn't be the last time.

Chapter 15
Knute Rockne Not Wanted

One thing that amazes me about American sports folklore is how soon it is forgotten among our youth. Several times in the junior high classroom, I would sometimes say, "Win one for the Gipper." Other times I would try to perk up my bored students with stories of the great Notre Dame football coach, Knute Rockne.

Most the time, their responses would be the same; who is the Gipper? Who is Knute Rockne? I'd always tell them about George Gipp and how his final words to Coach Rockne as he was dying of pneumonia was, "Tell the boys to go out there and FIGHT, FIGHT, FIGHT and win one for the Gipper."

Nobody knows if Gipp really said those words. Rockne had a way to motivate his players that might have stretched the truth. As Mark Twain once said, "Don't let the truth get in the way of a good story."

I read once Rockne asked his team to win a game for his young son, who was on his death bed back in South Bend, IN. They did win the game and when they returned home, Rockne's son met them at the airport. It must have been an amazing recovery.

Rockne was credited with many famous quotes. The one I like the best was, "Show me a good and gracious loser and I'll show you a failure." The coach died in a plane crash in the Flint Hills of Kansas but hopefully stories like I tell in my classroom will keep his legend alive.

There was no need for Rockne-like speeches and motivation during the 1982-1983 basketball season. Not only did we have superior talent going into most games, but the players seem to coach themselves. I was only 32 years old and didn't have much coaching experience, but it sure seemed easy.

The team could be laughing and clowning around right up until game time. But when the buzzer sounded to start the game, everyone was all business. After 33 years of coaching, I have never coached another team that could do that. How a bunch of 15 to 17 year old kids could be that mature is beyond me.

Even our bus driver was getting into the act. Her name was Deloris Broz and over the past seasons of driving for us, she had demanded no loud noises on the ride home, win or lose. Now, she seemed to enjoy listening to the celebrations of winning.

One tradition we started after the conference championship game was to learn and sing a song made popular by sixth grade teacher, Dave Newmyer. Dave was famous for leading all the people at wedding receptions with his version of Johnny Horton's hit, *Sink the Bismarck*. I had taught the team the words to the song. They would shout out the verses on the bus ride home after every win.

Maybe I shouldn't be surprised by the team's maturity. Every player on the varsity team in some way was inspired by the courage Brenda was showing in her fight against a deadly form of cancer. Even after it reappeared on her lungs, Brenda never slowed down in her support of her teammates.

Our only junior starter, Chris Packer knew exactly what Brenda was teaching her. "We all learned that it all could be gone in a moment. Brenda must have been born to give us that lesson. She bonded us together by the power of the human spirit. Our fight was to keep Brenda alive."

Now there only remained one step left before the Wilber-Clatonia team would qualify for their first state tournament appearance in history. A Clatonia boys' team had won the Class D championship in 1958. That team was anchored by Angie Miller's father, Oren. Now 25 years later, Angie's team had a chance to exactly match her dad's team with a 27 – 0 record. Only four games stood between the Wolverines and a perfect season.

That next step was our old nemesis, Centennial. The Wolverines had won two close games by five and three points. However, both had been in Centennial's gym. The Regional Tournament would be played at Milford Technical School. I really liked that location. I had lived in Milford for four years during my second teaching job in education.

I had a couple of friends who worked at the college and would help run the Regional Tournament. Bill Backes ran the gym and its intramural programs for the college. Leon Williams was an instructor and one of my closest friends during my time in Milford. I had coached his daughters in softball. Together, we had run a Memorial Day softball tournament that basically paid my summer salary, plus gave money to the ball programs.

Also, my first coaching mentor, Bob Bargen, was still in Milford. I spent two years as Bob's freshman coach. We spent a lot of time together coaching and scouting. It seemed we were always in a car scouting future opponents or at Bob's house talking basketball. I knew we would get first class treatment in Milford.

It was the end of February and the Wilber-Clatonia fans came out in droves to see if we could keep the unbeaten streak alive. The Centennial fans came in force, too. They were sure the third time was the charm in the series between the two teams. The Grant High School coach even flew in from the sandhills of Nebraska to scout the two teams. His team had already qualified for the state tournament.

The place was already jumping when I took the team, including Brenda, into the locker room for some final instructions. I had given those orders 23 times already, but this time I decided to give my best "win one for the Gipper" speech.

I'm not sure what I said, but I do remember yelling and throwing an eraser. The team charged out to battle like never before. So affective was my hell, fire and brimstone speech that my team that was averaging over 60 points per game scored two points in the first six minutes of the game. On top of that, one of the officials decided to call fouls really close and my post players were in foul trouble.

I called a time-out, regretting my locker room performance. I had to take it out on someone and the closest person was Tom Hood, the other official. I knew Tom well enough to know he wouldn't give me a technical foul.

The acoustics in the Milford Tech Gym were terrible. The Centennial band was blaring the fight song as I yelled at Tom, "That #*%! official is killing us!" Tom couldn't hear a word I said, so I repeated it. Tom shrugged his shoulders indicating he still couldn't hear me. I yelled it a third time, but just before I got to the #*%!, the band stopped playing and everyone heard what I said. It was the comic relief we all needed.

In truth, Centennial was more nervous than us. It took a while, but we wedged out a 50 – 41 win. I was very relieved to know my Knute Rockne impression hadn't cost us a win. I pledged never to do that again with this team.

I knew my friends from Milford would treat us well and they came through. Since Regionals is a single game, the nets usually stay safely in place. However, Leon and Bill had the ladder out on the court right after the game. They had heard about Brenda and her incredible courage and fight. Leon and Bill wanted to be part of that fight. Brenda cut down her third net of the season.

Wilber-Clatonia girls' basketball team was headed to the state tournament. Leon and Bill had one final surprise. I was ready to go to the bus for the 45 minute ride home when Leon stopped me and handed me the game ball. He asked me to give it to Brenda. I would do that, but at a very special time. We had a week to celebrate and then to Lincoln for the final three games of the season.

When the Nets Came Down for Brenda

Chapter 16
A Week of Records and <u>Recognition</u>

The Wilber-Clatonia girls' basketball team had a week to allow the jubilation of qualifying for their first state tournament. That was a good thing. The team also had time to realize their toughest job was just ahead.

While the Wolverines prepared for Hastings St. Cecilia in the quarterfinals Thursday afternoon at Pershing Auditorium, the two towns were gearing up for a big weekend in the capital city. Clatonia put a banner across Main Street, announcing the accomplishment to anyone who drove under it. The same type of banner had been strung up 25 years earlier when the undefeated Clatonia boys' team had made a state tournament appearance.

While the two high-scoring stars, Angie and Penny, were receiving most of the attention, the team knew there was a lot more to the success of the team. Beccy Duba, a senior starter realized the strength Brenda added to the team. "Brenda had a positive attitude and an infectious smile. I just hope she felt the same support from us that she gave to the team."

At a pep rally as the team boarded the bus for the 40 minute trip to Pershing Auditorium, Brenda received a special gift. The game ball from the Regional Tournament had been signed by all the players. As requested by Leon Williams and Bill Backes, the Regional Tournament hosts from Milford, Brenda was presented the game ball. It was a very special moment.

St. Cecilia had made several state tournament appearances and had at least one state championship. They had been one of the first towns to embrace AAU basketball for girls and their program had been one of the strongest in the state.

The Hawkettes came into the game with four losses and confidence from past state tournament appearances. The first half was up and down, with the Wolverines holding the early advantage. Robin Broz started the state tournament with a long range jumper. She did that in all three state tournament games.

Leading 30 – 22 with about five minutes left in the half, St. Cecilia made a run to take a 31 – 30 lead. Angie hit three free throws just before half and Wilber-Clatonia led by two at the break.

The third quarter, as it was almost always during the regular season, was dominated by the Wolverines. The lead expanded to 13 points halfway through the third quarter. Penny scored eight of her 16 points in that four minute period.

The lead increased to 17 points with 5:36 left in the game before St. Cecilia made a final surge. The Hawkettes closed to within seven points, but two steals and a pair of free throws from Renee Wickwire assured the Wolverines of a 67 – 58 win.

Angie was the big story. Despite being doubled teamed in the post, Angie scored a state tournament record 40 points. That set up a date with Grant High School. It was their coach who had flown into Lincoln to scout the Regional game in Milford.

However, there was a story equally as big as Angie's scoring record. Just to the left of Miller's game antics was a column in the Lincoln Star written by Randy York. It was titled, *Dedicated to Brenda*. It told the story that everyone in Wilber and Clatonia already knew. It described to all its readers the importance of a young sophomore at the end of the bench that never wore a uniform.

Dedicated to Brenda – Randy York, Sports Columnist

Thursday, Wilber won one for Brenda. Actually, the Wolverines have won 25 for Brenda.

This whole basketball season has been dedicated to the courageous little sophomore.

If you don't believe it, ask the five starters on Class C's top ranked girls team what they say when they're introduced before every game.

Ask them who they let cut down the net after the district final at Sterling.

Ask them who unraveled the last hook on the net at the regional playoff at Milford.

Ask them who was the star of Thursday morning's pep rally. It wasn't Gene Steinmeyer, their coach. It was Brenda Florian, the teammate who sat at the end of the bench Thursday afternoon, charting the shots she can no longer shoot.

Last November, Brenda intended to be out there, wearing the green and white of Wilber as proudly as anyone. She knew she faced a battle to play. But she never thought she'd be battling for her life.

When you're 16, you don't think about cancer.

But last December, surgeons at the Mayo Clinic amputated Brenda's leg 16 inches above her right knee to remove a malignant tumor. Last month, they removed five cancerous "seeds" in her right lung.

Wilber's drive to the state championship is almost over. Brenda's fight has only just begun.

She was special before

One thing should be emphasized. Cancer did not make Brenda Florian special. Her teachers, coaches and teammates knew she was special before it was ever diagnosed.

"She made our varsity basketball team as a freshman and had a good season on a good varsity volleyball team last fall," Steinmeyer said. "I didn't think her heart was in basketball again, though, so I sent her down to reserves after the first week of practice.

"Most kids would have taken that as a slap in the face," Steinmeyer said. "She told me I was right. She said she hadn't been giving basketball everything she had. But she said she'd work her way back up. And she would have. Brenda is that one kid in a hundred. She showed her quality and her guts before anyone even knew she had cancer."

Brenda's teammates have used that courage as a cue card. Dedicating every game to her was a spontaneous gesture and so far, it's been performed with prayers and hugs and without tears.

Last December, Brenda told her teammates that's the way she wanted it. But Thursday was tougher than any day in the last three months.

Before he Wolverines boarded the bus to leave for Lincoln and play Exeter (should have *been Hastings St. Cecilia), they gave Brenda a surprise. . . an autographed game ball from the regional championship.*

"I don't really put up a front. But sometimes, it's hard," Brenda said. "I try not to show anything to anybody. But it's getting harder. In the last week, I feel almost ready to give up."

Part of the despair is losing her hair from the first chemotherapy treatment a month ago. Part of it is knowing that she leaves Sunday morning for Mayo and another treatment on Monday.

"Right now, I'm kind of down in the dumps," Brenda admitted.

Even though cancer has helped her realize the relative insignificance of losing, Brenda still has her heart set on Wilber winning the championship.

"I'd like that last hook on that last net," she said.

"If we win, she'll be up there on the ladder," Steinmeyer said.

If the Wolverines don't win, they'll hug Brenda anyway.

They may even cry.

Brenda was no longer our secret weapon. Now everyone knew where the team's maturity and ability to perform under pressure originated. Now everyone knew about Brenda Florian.

When the Nets Came Down for Brenda

Chapter 17
<u>Then There Were Four</u>

  Reading Randy York's article in the paper Friday morning was emotional for me. I thought Randy had done a great job telling Brenda's story. It also made me face reality. The four teams left in Class C were very good teams. There was a chance Brenda may not get a chance to cut down the last net of the season.

  Grant had gone all out for the possible match-up with the number one team in the state. A rancher with an airplane had flown the Grant coach to watch the Regional game in Milford. It was a confident team from the Nebraska Sandhills that made the trip to Lincoln that first weekend in March.

  Back in Wilber, Brenda's mother wasn't sure if she should attend the game. Doris was the single mother of five children, although only two still lived at home. She now worked in the meat department of a mom and pop grocery store run by Paul Heller. Paul had been the principal at Wilber-Clatonia when I was hired four years earlier.

  Paul had been a former coach at Alma High School. He understood the importance of the games, not only for the students, but for the parents as well. He demanded that Doris take the time to attend the games. Even though Brenda would only keep statistics, Paul knew she was much more to the team than a statistic keeper. He also knew it was important that Doris experience the state tournament with her daughter.

The game began with Grant making a statement that they weren't intimidated by the 25 – 0 Wolverines. They jumped to a five point, first quarter lead. Then Grant extended the lead to 17 – 10 early in the second quarter. To make things worse, Penny was in foul trouble.

I remember very clearly hoping my team could keep the score under a 10 point deficit by halftime. I told my assistants, Dave Grothen and Jim Moore, exactly that. We would get Penny back after half-time and I felt we could make a comeback. Also, with Penny out of the game, the Grant defense could really gang up on Angie.

The lead grew to eight points late in the second quarter. With only 1:23 to go before intermission, it was still a six point lead when Angie took over. On two consecutive plays, Angie was able to isolate one on one with the Grant post player. Very few people in any class could match up with the record-setting senior.

Her last field goal came with only two seconds left in the half. Wilber-Clatonia trailed as they headed to the locker room, but only by two points. The maturity of the team really showed at halftime. Although Penny had three fouls and Angie had collected two, everyone was confident of stopping Grant in the second half. The team and Brenda had faced a lot tougher adversity than a mere two point deficit.

Penny immediately made her presence known by tying the score to open the second half. This time, however, the Grant wouldn't go away and hide. The lead see-sawed back and forth, with Grant taking a three-point lead at the midway point of the quarter. Wilber-Clatonia had regained a three-point lead with just over a minute left in the quarter, but Grant scored the final four points. Wilber-Clatonia had never trailed in the fourth quarter all year. Maturity would have to come through for them when the pressure was on.

With Penny leading the way, the Wolverines scored the first six points of the fourth quarter and maintained that lead for the first four minutes of the final quarter. Grant wasn't finished, though, and closed to within two points. Penny hit a free throw to give Wilber-Clatonia a three point cushion. Back in 1983, the three-point line was not a rule in high school basketball, so Grant would have to score twice to win the game.

Chris Packer, the starting point guard, had been very sick at the Regional game and her health hadn't improved much in the week before state. She gave it a go, but she just wasn't herself. Renee Wickwire, a 5-3 back-up point guard, played a lot of minutes for the ailing starter. Her moment to shine came with five seconds left in the game. Grant had hit a long-range field goal to cut the lead to one. They immediately fouled Renee. She coolly stepped to the line and hit both ends of the one and one to ice the win, finally.

I made the entire team stand by me for the final five seconds so there was no chance of a foul while Grant threw up a desperation shot. Even then, the Plainswomen turned it over as they threw it in-bounds. Penny had scored 16 of her 19 points in the second half. The entire Grant team had only scored 21 second half points. I told her during a time-out to just toss it to the Grant team and jump up and down, because we were on TV tomorrow. Despite being almost speechless in a television interview, Penny had proven she was a great player in her own right.

The championship game was at noon the next day. We hustled home to get some rest, if it was possible. Our opponent would be Omaha Cathedral, a full court pressing team. After getting the team back to Wilber, I hit the library to prepare a scouting report. I had a tape of Cathedral, but scouting was crude back then. I would find a play I wanted to show the team, then note what marker point the play occurred. I did the same with a tape of a popular movie. I had an idea for motivation that didn't include a "Win one for the Gipper" speech.

What I didn't mention was it was my birthday. Ironically, I share a birthday with Knute Rockne. That doesn't mean I should try his style of coaching.

My team was in the championship game. The preparations for Saturday were now complete. I wanted desperately to talk basketball with someone. As I drove through the streets of Wilber at about 11:00 pm, I found all the bars basically deserted.

I lived near Clatonia, so I headed to Rehm's tavern, owned by Dick Rehm, a friend of mine. I was shocked and disappointed to find it completely dark. My family deserted me, too. They had decided to spend the night in Lincoln so they wouldn't bother me. I went home and dove into a half gallon of ice cream; just me and my black lab, although I didn't share the ice cream. I knew I wouldn't get much sleep. We had a chance to get Brenda on that ladder for one final time.

When the Nets Came Down for Brenda

Chapter 18
The Final Net Comes Down

I don't remember if it was after the Grant game Friday evening or early Saturday morning, March 5, 1983. Whatever the time, I had the most important conversation of my short coaching career. My uncle, Gene Else, had been a high school and college basketball coach. He had coached the Clatonia boys' team in 1957 to a one-loss season. He gave up the reins that year, but most of the players give him credit for their 1958 state championship team.

I knew that Omaha Cathedral would run a tenacious, full court press against our team. We had lots of height, but wasn't a great ball handling team. My uncle suggested I use the strength of Angie and Penny to our advantage. He suggested that anytime we faced full-court defensive pressure, I have Penny take the ball out of bounds. She should find Angie around half-court. It was Angie's job to go get the ball. The guards were supposed to fly to front court as Angie looked to advance the ball.

In college basketball, shoot-arounds the day of the game is common. At Wilber-Clatonia, I had never held a shoot-around. At 9:00 am, March 5, the team would gather in the Wilber-

Clatonia gym for our first shoot-around. Brenda was there with the team. In the next 20 minutes, I put in the Gene Else-devised plan on breaking the press. I wasn't sure we could pull it off on such short notice. I really underestimated the maturity of this team.

Thirty minutes later, we were in the school library looking at the game tape of Omaha Cathedral that I had prepared the night before. I had unusual access to the library. Donna Mackey, the librarian, was very protective of her office area which was an enclosed pod in the center of the high school library. However, Donna's father was a very successful high school coach, so she knew the importance of this game. We all gathered around the television perched on a roll-cart. I would fast forward to the correct spots to show the team what to expect from the Omaha school.

Then it was time for my Knute Rockne idea. I had a copy of the movie, Rocky III. I loved all three of the Rocky's out by 1983. I had marked the spot where Rocky finally beats Apollo Creed and where Clubber Lang took severe punishment from a slimmed down Rocky Balboa. The team was so fired up after viewing the carnage; they almost tore the door off the library pod. Donna would have killed me.

As we headed for the capital city, we had one stop to make. Paul Heller had called me early Saturday morning with a personal request. The school bus was supposed to stop at the store before we left town. Waiting for us on Main Street were two cases of champagne. Of course, the champagne was non-alcoholic, but the symbolism was there. I just hoped it wasn't a premature celebration.

I faced one major problem as we neared Lincoln. The bus and its occupants were deadly quiet. Even Brenda and Lori didn't have much to say. I was really worried that nerves would cost us the championship. That's when Leah Carsten came to the rescue. Just as we entered the city limits, Leah began teasing Cheryl Wiese for getting caught parking with her boyfriend by the water tower in Wilber. That wasn't breaking any rules, but it might make Angie mad or disappoint Brenda, so Cheryl was denying the charges.

Just as we crossed the railroad tracks by the State Penitentiary, Leah, who was sitting at the back of the bus, told a joke about Cheryl, who was sitting toward the front. It was one of those jokes that appear to be a little off color at the beginning, but was innocent at the end. It was innocent if you didn't have a dirty mind, which we all did. The bus roared with laughter and the mood was broken. We got off the bus relaxed and laughing, thanks to Leah's insight.

I had made my mind up I would go easy on the motivational speeches. There would be no eraser throwing. I wouldn't mention the second round knockout of Clubber Lang. As the team got ready to take the court, we were delayed four or five minutes by television. The team didn't seem to mind too much. They spent the extra time singing Dave Newmyer's version of *Sink the Bismarck*. The people nearby had to think we were nuts, but we were ready for Omaha Cathedral.

Within the first two minutes of the game, every one of the starters had scored except Chris Packer. Chris had proven her worth by diving out of bounds to save an errant throw. It was 15 -2 before Cathedral knew what hit them. When I rested Angie or Penny, Cathedral's defense would force a few turnovers that narrowed the margin. However, I didn't allow that to happen very often. Despite the early scoring balance, this was a game for the two post players.

It was still fairly close at half with the Wolverines leading 33 – 26. Just like in past games, it was the third quarter that would settle the issue who was the best team in Class C. With Angie and Penny scoring on almost every possession, Wilber-Clatonia outscored Cathedral by 14 points in the third period. It was an insurmountable 21 point lead with only eight minutes left in the season. The lead climbed to 27 points as Angie and Penny continued to dominate the man defense of Cathedral.

Penny led the team with 29 points and Angie was close behind with 27 points. Their combined points outscored the entire Cathedral team by 10 points. The final score was 68 – 46.

All that was left was the post-game celebration. Channel 10 & 11 had broadcast the game to the entire state. After the game, it was tradition to interview the winning coach and a few players. I went first, followed by Angie and Penny, who actually proved they could talk on television. I have been told by many people they were impressed with the pair's humble interview.

Just as the television was ready to cut to a commercial, Jeff Small, the sportscaster doing the interviews, suddenly interrupted and asked me what was happening on the court. As I looked up, there was Brenda on top of the ladder proudly cutting down her fourth net of the season. I quickly told Brenda's story. Now everyone knew how important the kid at the end of the bench was to the state championship team.

Once in the locker room, the champagne was popped and the coaches were thrown in the shower. We snuck extra clothes into Pershing Arena just in case they were needed. We acted like we never wanted to leave. The second game of the day matched Shickley and Humboldt for the Class D title. It was almost over when we finally got on the bus for the victory ride back to Wilber. The bus driver never even complained when we failed to quiet down at the railroad tracks at the State Penitentiary. It was at that exact spot that Leah Carsten put her mark on the championship game late that morning.

There was a lot of celebrating that evening. The Carriage House in Clatonia provided the victory dinner for the team. Later, I headed to Rehm's tavern to continue the after-hours party, but only a few adults were there or even knew about it. Our goal was to stay at Rehm's Tavern, with the lights out, until the Lincoln Journal-Star newspaper was dropped off at about 4:00 am. The drop-off point was right across the steet.

We were pretty sleepy when the truck dropped off the papers. On the front of the sports section was a colored picture of Angie Miller as she scored two of her record 91 tournament points. Just a few columns away was a picture of a girl cutting down the nets. Brenda was smiling and waving the net in triumph. The sophomore who had such high hopes of being a small part of the team in November was now a major factor in the March successes; and she hadn't even suited up.

When the Nets Came Down for Brenda

Chapter 19
The Match Maker

The fight for perfection was over, but Brenda's fight was just getting started. Right after the state championship game, Brenda went back to the Mayo Clinic for more treatments and surgery. The seeds kept appearing on her lungs.

That didn't mean there weren't typical times for a 16-year old high school sophomore. It was during a fundraiser for Brenda that she pulled her magic as a couple's match-maker.

A dance had been arranged at Sokol Hall in Wilber. There would be live music by local musicians. Businesses in town had helped with the expenses. Brenda's brother, Brian, had moved back from York and Brenda thought he needed a girlfriend. This fundraiser provided the perfect setting.

Brenda arranged for Brian to meet Judy Odvody. She thought they would make a great couple. Brenda let Judy know about her plans for the meeting. "She wanted me to meet Brian," Judy said. "I thought he was really tall. When Brenda asked what I thought, I told her, 'Oh, I don't know, he's tall.'"

It must not have bothered Judy too much. Maybe it was Brenda's insistence about how her brother and Judy would make an excellent match. Whatever the reason, sparks flew. They dated and eventually married.

Doris saw the ability of matching compatible couples in her daughter. "Brenda was a match-maker," Doris said. "Ginger (Zajicek) would call and talk to her about all her boyfriend troubles. I started calling Brenda Dear Abby. Her friends would call her to gather information about their boyfriends or girlfriends."

It was important to Brenda to see her older siblings in good relationships. She wrote to Lori about Arlene's husband, Scott Albert. *"It was fun; Scott and me sat on one side of the table and talked, while Arlene, Mom, Missy and Granny sat on the other side and talked. He's a real neat guy and I like him a super lot. I feel like I'm lucky to have him as a bro-in-law."*

About the time the knee began to hurt, Brenda hooked up with an older high school student. In the fall of 1982, Randy Kalkwarf and Brenda began to date. Randy was a senior, two years older. The cancer didn't drive Randy away.

"She first told me after class about the cancer," Randy remembered. "She was crying about it. It drew us a lot closer. She was a strong girl."

It was tough for Brenda to be separated from her friends when she made her monthly trips to the Mayo Clinic. Brenda wrote to Lori Kreshel, *"Gosh darn, I miss Randall so much already and it's only been two days! Make sure you keep an eye on him for me, OK? Make sure he stays out of trouble."*

Randy graduated in 1983 and started school at Milford Technical College that summer. Thanks to Brian's mentoring, Brenda could drive a car with an automatic transmission by herself. She would take her mother's car to see Randy in Milford. It was less than an hour's drive, but you had to maneuver through 10 miles of gravel roads.

One night especially worried Doris. "We had that big brown Chevy," Brenda's mother said. "She would go to Milford and see Randy. One night it was so foggy and I was so worried about her. Of course, we didn't have cell phones then."

"I called Randy and he said she left a long time ago. I waited another 15 minutes and here she came. She had her leg amputated. That's why I was so worried. She had gone by herself and it was foggy and this big, old car. . ."

Brenda used her time with Randy to put cancer out of her mind, if only for a short time. "At times it was really tough," Randy said. "We got along so well. We didn't talk about stuff like the cancer. She tried to forget. We even talked about getting married and having kids. It helped keep her mind off the cancer."

Brenda discussed the possibility of marriage with her mother. "Brenda, you have to think if you got married, can Randy take care of you, pay all the doctor's bills, and all this?" Doris asked.

"If I don't get married and I can't have the most beautiful wedding," Brenda told her mother. "I'll have the most beautiful funeral." Brenda would do just that.

Marrying his girlfriend in the face of huge medical bills didn't seem to faze Randy. "I loved her that much." Randy said. "I just wanted to be with her. She was my life. She stuck with me, too. I wanted to make her happy in the time she had left."

Brenda resigned herself that she would not experience married life. She would never have children. She did continue to worry about Randy. "Bird, I really need you right now," Brenda wrote to Lori. "Randy hurts real bad!" Brenda never stopped taking care of her friends.

Chapter 20
<u>Protecting Mom</u>

Doris Florian is no wilting flower. Doris is one tough lady even if life hasn't always been fair. It began with five healthy children. First two boys were born, Alan being the oldest, and the drag racer, Brian coming next. Brenda enjoyed hanging out with her older brothers' distractions like cars and music.

Three girls came next for the Doris and Jerome Florian. Arlene was the middle child, followed by Brenda and last but not least, Melissa. It was a great family of five that lived in Ord. It was then that Jerome's kidneys began to fail.

That made a move to Wilber necessary. Doris organized her family to survive the hardships that came with Jerome's disabilities. The whole family always was on the go to make ends meet. Jerome had a kidney transplant and experienced a period of decent health.

Then on August 22, 1978, Jerome's transplanted kidney failed. Brenda lost her father and Doris lost her husband. She was now a single parent.

Doris' children grew and gradually left the house. By 1982, Alan, Brian and Arlene had all left to pursue their careers. However, in December the unthinkable would happen. Cancer was found on Brenda's right leg and she would have to fight like her father did for all those years. Life was about to throw Doris another curve.

Brenda was aware of all the sacrifices her mother had made for the family. Only 16 years old, Brenda was determined to protect her mom. "There were several times we were in the doctor's office and she wanted me to leave," Doris said. "She didn't want me to stay there. I know she was pinning down the doctors on how long she had left and what she could expect. I didn't know until later."

Doris continued to work for Paul Heller at the grocery store. Brenda was always in her thoughts. "During the summer, I'd call home. Melissa told me she was sleeping on the couch. She hid how sick she was from me. I had a hard time keeping track of her."

Brenda protected her mother from some of the realities of her disease. However, she openly expressed how she felt about her mom. "She would write on the mirror," Doris explained. "She would put "I love you, Mom," or "Happy birthday, Mom." She worried about me."

Brenda would write on the mirror with a bar of soap. Her messages were printed in huge print on the mirrors. When she wrote, "I Love You Mom!" the "o" in love would be in the shape of a heart. Those special words would cover the entire mirror, with a huge exclamation point after "Mom."

The "Happy Birthday, Mom!" came with a decorated mirror. Brenda would put decorative paper of different colors around her special message.

All this pales in comparison to the message Brenda wrote to her mother in a Christmas card. The card read, *"It's love like yours that makes happy families like ours."* However, it was the personal message that really expressed all of Brenda's love for her mother.

"Mom – Christmas time is a time for love and joy. I'm writing you to tell you that I love you so much, much more than I ever express."

"I've put you through so much, Mom. Although none of us can do anything about it – and sometimes I feel as though it's my fault. I know it isn't. If this is what God wants, this is what we have to give him. You've done so much for me and I have grown a lot from my experience. I'm sorry I have to put you through

what I am. If I could only change it, I would, but I can't. And I'm so sorry."

"We'll all be happy and live our lives to the fullest! We don't know what the future brings; maybe it will bring us joy; maybe it will bring us sadness, but no matter what, God takes what he wants, and no matter what we do, we can't stop him."

"I love you very much, Mom, and I always will!"

Chapter 21
<u>The Right Stuff</u>

When Brenda's cancer made its fateful appearance, the person most mentally equipped to handle such a catastrophic situation probably was Brenda. She had been very close to her father who had been ill for years. Also, Brenda's cousin, Lisa Albert, died very quickly from leukemia.

Arlene and Brian provided family support and her mother gave unconditional love. However, most of Brenda's teachers, her fellow classmates, and other adults didn't provide much support. They were understandably afraid of the situation. They didn't know what to say or how to handle the situation. Most disappeared from Brenda's life when she needed them the most.

I'm afraid I wasn't much better. I would like to jump up and take a lot of credit for the net-cutting ceremonies during the magical, championship basketball season. I really don't think I had much to do with it. I helped order the bumper stickers for Brenda, but I'm pretty sure it was the team who thought up that idea.

It really wasn't until the 1983-1984 basketball season that I began to understand what made Brenda so unique. I remember very clearly the first conversation I had with Lori Kreshel about the truth of Brenda's cancer. Before that moment, I was in denial about the life and death struggles ahead for Brenda.

I was taping Lori's ankle before practice. Lori had broken her ankle at basketball camp at Midland College during the summer. It caused her to miss her entire junior year of volleyball. She was able to play basketball, but the ankle required support.

Innocently, I inquired about Brenda, who had been missing most of the games and a lot of school. As casually as if we were talking about boyfriends, Lori was very open with her conversations with Brenda of death and heaven. I was really shocked at her honesty.

There were, however, a couple of teachers at Wilber-Clatonia that had the right stuff to emotionally help the seriously ill teenager. Dennis Potthoff was the boys' basketball coach and a high school history teacher. No one knew just how well equipped Dennis was to deal with Brenda's situation.

Dennis attended Palisade High School in western Nebraska. During his senior year, he dealt with the death of a student. "I was on the student council," Dennis said. "There was a kid in third or fourth grade that had Cystic Fibrous.

That year she died. The student council got into fund raising. I got involved in that work."

"It was the first time I had to grapple with kids dying. I didn't really have any deaths in my family before then."

Dennis had been teaching for four years before 1983. Suddenly, memories flooded back. "It took me back to the emotion of Glenda (the Palisade fourth grader)," he said. "I had a sense that life is really unfair. This is a great kid. She's really sick and she might not get better. It was a reminder that every day is precious."

"I have one fuzzy memory. Brenda and I had a conversation sitting at a table. I remember her being there. She cried a little bit. It was early in her illness and she was scared. I told her I believed there's some kind of purpose for your life. She was very faithful for a kid that age."

Now a department chair for the College of Education at the University of Nebraska – Kearney, Dennis was emotional at times as he recalled his time with Brenda. "Kids are way smarter than adults," he said. "Brenda was really strong. Most parents and teachers weren't strong and they were scared."

A positive line of communication with Brenda is how Dennis dealt with the situation. "Why talk about being sick?" Dennis said.

"That's the way I approached it. You don't know how you'll respond until you are there. I just wanted to be there for her. It doesn't help to feel sorry for her."

"When Brenda found herself in this position, she fought. Brenda played it out gracefully until the end. She knew this was it. She was very strong but graceful. I was mostly humbled and embarrassed. We're going to fight this sucker. Most people think you can't die at age 16. I learned that kids teach adults about death."

Dennis had gained valuable information from Glenda, the dying girl in Palisade. His knowledge helped him connect with Brenda. She now had an adult who would listen and understand. "With situations like Brenda, I'm just one teacher," Dennis said. "But which teacher will step up? It was just two people on the planet. You don't know why the connection happens. The early experience I had in high school gave me a script in high school."

"Sometimes you just get tapped on the shoulder. I think she was blessed. She was a fighter. At some point, she realized that the fight wasn't the issue. You play out the string the best you can."

Chapter 22
Now We Are Juniors

The summer of 1983 was over and the two best friends were ready to enter their junior year of high school. They did all the things most juniors would do. Both Lori and Brenda had boyfriends. Their conversation often headed in that direction.

Like most kids with cars, the pair loved to cruise Main Street of Wilber. Often they went in Lori's big, yellow car. It was because of that car Lori was given her nickname, Big Bird. The nickname was in reference to the car and the Muppets character, Big Bird, who was as yellow as Lori's car.

Lori had sprained her ankle in basketball camp that summer. However, it never healed and in late August, Dr. Travnicek discovered it was broken. Trav put a cast on Lori's ankle, informing her she would have to wear it until mid-October.

That meant Lori would miss her junior season of volleyball. "Isn't it interesting?" Lori said. "I couldn't go out for volleyball my junior year, either. So Brenda and I both went to the games and we sat in the bleachers, having fun, marveling that we were both benched."

The best friends may have sat in the bleachers, but more than likely they sat on the varsity bench as their teammates competed that fall of 1983. "When someone's sick on your team, you have a whole new sense," Lori said. I didn't like volleyball and Brenda loved volleyball. Brenda and I sat on the bench the whole volleyball season. She was grateful for that."

"Brenda and I would go to games. She was sick for 18 months. That killed her not to play. That's where we were recognized; we were huge. None of us were very good, but we had the heart and desire."

In a letter to Brenda, Lori made the most of her injury. *"Anyway chicko, with this stupid ankle of mine, it looks like I'll be at the Florian house an awful lot of the time; yes, yes, yes! Now there's 2 hop-a-longs. (And yes, mine IS more noticeable than yours!!) Jerk; ha, ha."*

Lori explained her feeling about the lost volleyball season in a letter to her God Daughter and niece, Gina Albert, who is Arlene's daughter. *"At first I felt sorry for myself. But it was such a blessing for Brenda and me. You see, Brenda LOVED volleyball and that junior year she could not play, for obvious reasons. Well, instead of having to watch all her friends play, I was out for the season and I sat around with her during each game. We helped with stats and basically had fun."*

Lori's ankle healed by basketball season. However, with the top four scorers, including All Stater's Angie and Penny, lost to graduation, expectations were not real high for the Wolverines. Lori and her teammates had other ideas.

In another letter to Gina, Lori wrote, *"The next year was supposed to be a "building year." Gene Steinmeyer was still our coach and not much was expected of us since Angie and Penny had graduated."*

"But Cheryl (Wiese) and I had learned a lot from our former teammates and a lot of the offense was built around having two posts. You see, not many teams in small-town Nebraska have tall players. We had not one, but two."

Led by Ginger Zajicek, the two post players, Lori and Cheryl, and the two feisty guards, Chris Packer and Renee Wickwire, the Wolverines won 14 of their first 16 games. Their only losses were to Class D powerhouse, Adams. Adams featured a freshman guard, Trudi Veerhusen, who would later play for me at Doane College.

Lori knew there was another force pushing the team to success. In the same letter to Gina, she wrote, *"Plus we had Brenda. She was no longer able to play, but man, did she ever root us on. She continually asked me to make nine points a game for her."*

"If I played well, she congratulated me. If I played lousy, she listened like a good friend, then she'd urge me to try harder. She asked me to practice an extra 15 minutes each day, just for her."

In the 16th game of the season, Brenda must have thrown a party for Lori. She scored 17 points in the team's 14th win of the season over Odell. It was the third highest total for a team member in the 1983-1984 season.

The team went into a small slump, losing two games in a row to Milford and Hebron. However, they rebounded with an amazing 56 – 51 win over old rival, Centennial. Centennial had returned basically their whole team from the year before.

The Wolverines had been beaten in the first round of the conference tournament. However, they would get their chance at a championship in the district and regional tournaments at Doane College.

Wilber-Clatonia raced past Southern and Tri County and then avenged their loss to Milford by beating them 50 – 35 in the Regional Tournament. No nets were cut down this year, however. The Nebraska State Activities

Association had combined the boys' and girl's events. With a boys' game to follow, no ladders were sent to the court after our win. The boys' game had to start on time.

That experiment lasted only one year. It did, however, eliminate one of the most special memories of the previous season.

In a year that was more unpredictable than the championship year, the group of substitutes from the previous year finished with a 19 – 5 record. The Lincoln Journal-Star had them ranked 5th and the Omaha World Herald put us 7th best in Class C-1. Not bad for a bunch of unknowns, inspired by a girl with one leg.

Ginger had a great season and was named to the All-State second team. She also was selected to play in the Coaches' All Star Game in August. Ginger, along with Renee, Cheryl and Chris had all won some post-season honors.

There was one very troubling fact. Brenda's fight was just about over.

When the Nets Came Down for Brenda

Chapter 23
<u>This is It</u>

The years have warped my memory on how much Brenda was able to be a physical presence with the 1983-1984 basketball team. We all knew that she had to make frequent trips to the Mayo Clinic.

Then there were the four surgeries to remove the cancerous seeds from her lungs. Brenda also continued chemotherapy treatments. She was often too sick to even attend school. She was, however, always there for her friends.

Lori would report to Brenda on how she played each game. Brenda had set a goal of Lori averaging 9 points per game. By the end of the season, Lori had almost accomplished it by scoring 174 points, a 7.25 point per game average. More importantly than the points, Lori was becoming a team leader.

Despite Brenda's cancer, the pair often spoke of the future. In another letter to Gina, Lori's God Daughter, Lori wrote, *"When Brenda and I were growing up together, we spent hundreds of hours discussing our future husbands and our children. Each boy that struck our interest was put into the role of husband, if only,* momentarily. *We would day dream and wonder and like any normal boy-crazed teen, created a world of blissful happily-ever after for ourselves."*

Lori had a paper route in the mornings before school. Often, she would find a letter waiting for her at the Florian house that Brenda had written the night before. In one of those letters, Brenda wrote, *"I decided tonight, I wanted to go to college for beauty (I need it). You know, cutting hair, etc. Don't let me forget, I'll tell you about it when I get back! I'm excited!"*

The special relationship the two shared gave Lori a deep insight. "We just had fun together," Lori said. "What do you do with your friend?"

"As a Catholic, one of the things I admired about her and that affected me the most was sacrificial living. She would say she would give it up for God. She just kept offering it up. Life is not about our legs, it's not about our breasts, it's not about her hair. She just got that. Looking back, that's what affected me the most was her grasp of that."

Bonnie, Lori's mother, worried about her daughter. She was afraid of the affect such a close relationship with a dying friend would have on Lori. It was the maturity of a 16 year old, high school junior that put Bonnie's mind at rest. Lori asked her mom if she would want Brenda to desert her if she had cancer.

Brenda worried about Lori, too, as shown in one of her letters to her best friend. *"I just feel like sometimes you're too good for me and I don't want to be your friend because of it."*

"I mean, sure everyone has their talents. Yours is singing, SMARTNESS, and basketball, things like that. I mean let's face it. I am not smart (and I hate working for good grades) and I can't sing. I have no other talents. I can't even walk sexy!"

Sometime after the first of the year, the doctors told Brenda that they couldn't stop the cancer. They were no longer able to surgically remove the seeds from her lungs. Brenda always asked her mom to leave the doctor's office so she could get total honesty from them. They knew this brave teenager deserved the truth about her illness.

It was time to break the news to her best friend. I'm sure picking the right moment was difficult for Brenda. Lori would never forget where she was when Brenda gave her the devastating news.

In a letter to Gina, Lori wrote, *"I was in eleventh grade history class* (note: Dennis Potthoff's class) *sitting by Brenda. She had a bandana around her head because she hated her wig. She looked at me and said, 'Well, Bird, this is it. The ol' docs told me I have two to three months to live.'"*

"I sat there, reeling. What? Brenda was going to die? For sure? I kept thinking, she can't tell me this monumental news while we're sitting in class together."

Brenda had tried to spare her mother from some of the truths her doctors revealed. Now it was time to share reality with her mother.

"She told me one day," Doris said. "Mom, we're going to talk about this. I don't want you to cry. I'll be okay because I'll be with Daddy in heaven."

"What could I do? Sit there and cry? She worried about me."

The final chapter to Brenda's young life was about to unfold. However, she refused to curl up and die. She was determined to live her final months to the fullest. The most inspirational part of Brenda's journey was about to open up.

Chapter 24
Wishes Granted

Just about the time Brenda was cutting down the final net after the 1983 State Championship game, a group of people were about to incorporate a foundation with a new idea. The idea was a way to raise money to grant wishes for terminally ill children.

The Make-A-Wish Foundation, today a household name, was in its early stages of growth in 1983. John Aalborg from Lincoln was touched by what Make-A-Wish did from a story he saw on television. John approached his friend, Scott Nelson, about the new charity.

Carol Jorde from Omaha had lost a son to cancer. A man had granted her son a wish before he died, although the individual wasn't part of Make-A-Wish. After hearing about Make-A-Wish, Carol wanted to get a Nebraska chapter going. The three heard about each other and began organizing the Make-A-Wish Foundation in Nebraska.

The first thing the new corporation had to do was establish a board of directors. Fourteen people were named. Randy York, the Lincoln Journal-Star sports writer, and Dr. Mark

Hutchins, M.D., were two of the founding board members.

Randy had written the touching column about Brenda during the State Tournament in 1983. Dr. Hutchins was a pediatrician and one of his patients was Brenda Florian. Both of these men knew and had been touched by Brenda's strength and courage. They helped make Brenda the first person to have her wish granted by Make-A-Wish in Nebraska.

That's not entirely true. Five-year old Shawna Arehardt had asked to see her aunt in Phoenix, AZ. Tony Perkins was 12 years old. He wanted to go to Sea World before cancer took his life.

Make-A-Wish had set up all the arrangement for both youth. Unfortunately, both entered the hospital and died just days before their planned trip. Fortunately, Tony did get a couple of wishes granted. While in the hospital, Mr. T, Rocky Balboa's adversary in the movie, Rocky III, sent an autograph. Tom Landry, the Dallas Cowboys coach, wrote a personal note, and Irving Fryer, a wide receiver for the Nebraska football team came to visit Tony. He even dedicated a game in Tony's memory.

At the beginning of the spring in 1984, Make-A-Wish was ready to grant their second official wish. Brenda's mother remembers how things unfolded. "I remember going to the Make-A-Wish place in Lincoln," Doris said.

"They told her she could go where ever she wanted. She wanted to ski but the high elevation and the fact she needed oxygen stopped that trip. She picked Orlando."

On March 18, 1984, Brenda and younger sister, Melissa flew to Disney World in Orlando. Of course, Doris was with them, too. The trip almost shut down before it could get started. "When we got down there, Brenda couldn't breathe," Doris recalled. "I called the doctor back in Lincoln. I wanted to come home and told him she's having a terrible time."

The doctor Doris called was Dr. Hutchins, a board member of Make-A-Wish. "He said that she should stay and for me to calm down," Doris said. "He called a doctor down there and they got oxygen to her. I remember going back to the room and Mickey Mouse came in. She barely remembered it because she couldn't breathe."

However, once Brenda started on the oxygen, the trip went much smoother. "It was wonderful," Doris said. "Everywhere we went, we got first class service."

Brenda even checked one more thing off her bucket list while in sunny Florida. "Brenda wanted to lie out on the beach," Melissa recalled. "It was cold and we had to wear sweatshirts, but we went down to the beach."

Soon after Brenda's leg was amputated in late 1982, she began to correspond through the mail with the Governor of Nebraska, Bob Kerrey. Governor Kerrey, who would later make a run at the presidency, had an artificial leg as result of an injury sustained in Viet Nam. Brenda and the Governor had something to talk about.

Brenda had a second wish; to meet the Governor of Nebraska. Governor Kerrey wanted to meet Brenda, too. It was arranged that Brenda would have lunch at the Governor's Mansion after they returned from Orlando.

However, Brenda went to the hospital in Lincoln. There she received her final chemotherapy treatment. "Governor Kerrey came to the hospital to see her," Doris said. "All the nurses knew he was coming. They were all looking at the stairs, waiting for him."

"Kerrey comes and he has a security person with him. He had on jeans and a T-shirt. He walked in the room and he was visiting with Brenda. Brenda didn't need me so I walked out of the room."

Probably because of the year-long correspondence or maybe just because she was Brenda, the conversation went into the personal life of Governor Kerrey. In 1984, the divorced

Governor Kerrey was dating actress Debra Winger, having met when she filmed *Terms of Endearment* in Lincoln.

"I went back in and asked how did the visit go?" Doris said. "Brenda was laughing and she said, "I asked him how his love life was?" Governor Kerrey said, "We don't see each other much, but we write mushy letter to each other."

Brenda wasn't through drilling Governor Kerrey. "Then Brenda asked him about his ex-wife. He said she was down south and he would get the kids in the summertime. You know, Brenda wouldn't spare any words. She wanted to meet him because she knew he had an artificial leg. I'm sure the two of them talked about that, but she had to ask him about Debra Winger."

After the chemotherapy treatment and Brenda regained some strength, the gutty teenager headed back home in Wilber. The future may be short, but there was a prom and Brenda had every intention of being at the event. There was other planning to do, also.

When the Nets Came Down for Brenda

Chapter 25
<u>Is There a Heaven?</u>

Death would take Brenda, an unfortunate certainty. The final chemotherapy treatment had been administered. A hospital bed had been brought to the Florian house. The teenager, with cancer spreading from her lungs to her brain, was now on oxygen. However, she remained amazingly strong.

Brenda, more than ever, turned to her best friend, Lori for answers to life's toughest questions. "It was the best conversation of my life," Lori said. "We talked non-stop about life and death."

"What do you think about heaven? What's going to happen? Am I going to see Dad? Is he going to recognize me? Is there a tunnel? Is there a light? When you die, what do you do? Are there angels? That's all we talked about."

"We would try to piece it together. I would read the Bible, trying to find bits and pieces. We were reading the Guide Post, all these different things. There were some stogie, Catholic farts trying to do some weird things. We were just praying."

The questions were being asked by a pair of high school juniors. I look back and the strength and courage that Brenda displayed amazed me. At the time, I knew that Lori was giving very special support for her friend. However, the depth of Lori's care in those final months may be considered miraculous.

Lori provide invaluable friendship and counseling for Brenda. She stayed late at basketball practice, trying to live up to all Brenda's expectations. Lori never stopped being an excellent student. Cheryl Wiese, her basketball teammate and classmate, matched Lori grade-for-grade all through high school.

I only knew tiny pieces of the events of those final months. I gained most my knowledge from short conversations with Lori. As the final games of the 1983-1984 basketball season were played, Lori would offer small glimpses into Brenda's struggle; the constant quest to find answers to questions that had no clear cut explanations. Brenda and Lori would have to dig deep into their faith to find what they were looking for.

"The thing I cherished the most was once she was told she was going to die, she'd say, 'Is there a heaven? Tell me there's a heaven.' We would just sit together and ponder this," Lori said.

"She wanted to remain pure," Lori explained. "It was kind-of an obsession. She wanted to remain pure for God. Once she knew she was going to die, we talked about God almost non-stop. Almost every time we were together, she would ask me a question or I would ask her a question."

The spring of 1984 was cool and rainy. Brenda loved to spend time on her front porch. The weather didn't stop her. She especially loved to visit on the porch when the sun was out to keep her warm.

"The most poignant memories are the ones where Brenda and I are sitting on her front porch," Lori said. "We would talk about death, looking up at the blue sky, wondering where she'd be once she died. Is there a heaven? Yes! How can we know for sure? What will happen to me once I die? Where will I go exactly?" Answers were slowly coming for the pair of truly incredible, young girls.

Brenda loved butterflies. She often pasted clip-art butterflies on the letters she wrote to Lori. That led to another discussion about death and beyond. "She started thinking about things like a metamorphous," Lori said. "She kept thinking like a butterfly. She thought about a change that's not going to be final because death is final."

Somehow, the discussions always went back to their Catholic faith. "Brenda wrote in a letter, *"I am a light and I'll never stop burning,"* Lori said. "We read this in a Reader's Digest or a Catholic Digest. It was a little article about our light that never goes out. That gave her such comfort."

I still can't believe the strength and insight that Brenda and Lori carried during those final months, weeks, and days. The old saying, "If I only knew then what I know now," really applies for me. I was Lori's coach, but she was a much more important coach to her best friend.

I even think Lori is astounded by their actions so many years ago. "That's kind-of where we were," Lori said. "I look back and I think holy crap!"

Chapter 26
The Most Beautiful Funeral

Most girls dream about their wedding day. Cancer did not wipe away that dream for Brenda. She still wanted to find the perfect man, the perfect wedding day, and the perfect setting. As her life drew to a close, she changed her focus.

"She was really, really sick," Doris said. "She realized she wouldn't get married. She told me that if she couldn't have the most beautiful wedding, she'd have the most beautiful funeral. Brenda starting planning with the same passion for her funeral she would have used on her wedding.

Brenda surprised Lori with her plan to organize her funeral. "She told me she was doing a cool thing in planning her funeral," Lori said. "I want everyone to cry their eyes out," Brenda told Lori. "I want the best and most glorious funeral."

One of the first jobs was finding her pallbearers. She selected Gordie Vlasak, Russ Kalkwarf, Kirk Ripa, Darin Keller, Darrell Korinek and Cary Stahl. They were invited to the Florian living room without a single idea what was about to happen.

Lori wrote about the experience in a letter to Gina. *"The funniest experience was when she gathered four or five guys in her living room with the intention of asking them to be her pallbearers. They all came to her house and she kept smiling at them, not sure of how to go about asking them her important question.*

She finally asked me if I'd do it. I looked at them and said, "Brenda wants to know if you'd be pallbearers at her funeral." I remember them sitting there, astounded and flabbergasted.

She teased them about not dropping her, etc. They did not know how to respond. Finally, they each said yes and shuffled out of the house. Wasn't Brenda amazing?"

Doris remembers Gordie Vlasak and Russ Kalkwarf when they heeded Brenda's request for a visit. "The boys came down to visit Brenda and she asked them," Doris recalled. "Gordie took it pretty hard for a long time afterwards, too. When he would see me, it crossed his mind."

Brenda bought a purple dress for the prom. She would be buried in that dress. She wanted to be buried in a white coffin. The location where she wanted to be buried was an easy decision. "My husband (Jerome) is here (Wilber) and I will be here," Doris said. She wanted to be buried there. They told her there wasn't room, but they found room. She had everything planned."

Dennis Potthoff had been a teacher Brenda could confide in as the cancer attacked her body. Dave Grothen, Brenda's basketball coach, had been there for her as well. Lori Connot, a business teacher at Wilber-Clatonia, became one of the few adults that connected with Brenda.

Lori (Connot) became very close to Brenda. She credits lessons learned from her father, ironically a retired basketball coach, for giving her the tools to deal with her dying student.

Lori also credits Brenda for giving her a life lesson. "I didn't think I would learn so much from a student," she said. "They hadn't taught me about what to do in that situation in college. I was prepared for some of it."

"Brenda was so mature. We talked a lot. She wanted me to help her plan her funeral. It was amazing talking so openly with this girl. Her dad's death was so close to her own. I was learning while I was going through it."

"When it got closer to when she was dying, she told me she wished the kids would understand the importance of the little things. I tell my kids about her."

Her best friend, Lori, said Brenda didn't miss any details. "She chose all her music," She wanted all these different things and all these things she could control."

"She talked to me about being pure myself and leading a better life. She taught me not to worry about what people think of me."

Finally, the planning was complete. Then Lori had a request from Brenda. "I kept telling her I wanted one last letter," Lori said. "Brenda told me she wasn't going to write one last letter."

"If I had written her a last letter, I would have written *I wish I would be on my way to meet God. You are in a much better position than I ever will be. You have been anointed. You will meet the Lord. How I envy you. Don't be scared or anxious. You'll be in a better place. In heaven it will be all good with no pain. I wish I could go.*"

Chapter 27
The Last Bucket

The last time I visited Brenda, it was a sunny, April afternoon. Jim Moore and I sat with her at her favorite spot, the front porch. Doris told me I came to visit Brenda occasionally, but I only remember the last one.

Brenda told us about the Orlando trip to Disney without giving a hint on how close it came to being cancelled. The thing I remember most was her plans later that week. She was going to Lincoln to buy a prom dress. The prom was just around the corner and Brenda had every intention of wearing a purple dress for the occasion.

The porch was the visiting center of the Florian house. Brenda had forced Dave Grothen to talk to her when she took off her prosthesis on his desk at school. They were close now, and Dave's memory of his last visit was the front porch, too.

Brenda wanted to do something else at her favorite visiting spot. "She wanted to drink beer on the front porch," Lori said. It was a dying girl's wish and Doris let the pair do just that. On a sunny, spring day the pair of best friends stretched out and enjoyed a few suds, just like their older mentors.

Lori wrote about the experience in a letter to Gina. *"It was such an odd feeling, because drinking was prohibited to teens, of course. Yet we just laughed at that rule and sat down in broad daylight and drank beer with much enjoyment."*

Oscar Wilde, the Irish writer and poet of the late 1800's said, "No good deed goes unpunished." The simple bucket list of Brenda Florian would take an almost comical turn. The long-time high school science teacher, Dennis Zlab, lived at a diagonal from the Florian's front porch. He observed Brenda and Lori snubbing their nose at the drinking rule. He reported what he observed to the Wilber-Clatonia High School administration.

Lori wrote what happened next. *"The administration did not know what to do with us. What do you do to someone who's going to die when they are drinking beer? Take them out of a sport they don't even participate in? Suspend them from a school they can no longer attend due to weakness? We kind of had the school between a rock and a hard place."*

The school principal, Ernie Talarico, made sure a sensible solution was made. "Mr. Talarico and the board (of education) chose to ignore it,"

Lori said. "He honored Brenda. I thought that was very cool."

Despite the sadness that goes when a young person is dying, Brenda found humor in an event during her final days. Brenda remained strong through the weekend. On Saturday night, she turned to her brother, Brian, and asked to go cruising.

Brian and Brenda were close, partly due to Brian's love of cars. It was Brian who taught Brenda to drive with one leg. The siblings jumped in Brian's car for a cruise around the streets of Wilber. When they got home, Brenda was angry.

Earlier, a male classmate of Brenda's had sought out her advice. The boy had a physical problem and related to Brenda's plight. Not everyone was happy with the meeting. The young man's girlfriend took offense. "They (Brian and Brenda) were out cruising," Doris explained. "This girl gave Brenda the finger. Brenda came home and she was mad. Can you imagine her being jealous of Brenda?" The dying girl's popularity could still trigger a reaction.

Brenda had a special request for Sunday. She wanted a special meal of fried chicken, mashed potatoes, and gravy. For dessert was Brenda's favorite, mayonnaise cake. That Sunday morning, Doris cooked for Brenda.

"I didn't go to church because she would have been left alone," Doris said. "I didn't know death was that close, but she slept all day so she didn't eat much. For some reason, my brother, Larry, came to visit. He brought pizza or something. That whole day, she didn't wake up much."

Unfortunately, death was close. Brenda had spent her final days at her favorite spot or doing one of her favorite activities. Sleep came easy on Sunday. Monday would be a day of great sadness.

Chapter 28
<u>Did Someone Say I was Dying?</u>

Lori knew that Monday would be Brenda's last day on the planet. She wanted to be by Brenda's side to say goodbye to her best friend. Yet still, Lori went to school with a great deal of apprehension.

"They called me from school," Lori said. "Mr. Talarico said Brenda was dying and I needed to go and say goodbye. I ran into the house and she was sitting up."

Brenda then said something Lori would never forget. "Do you think I'm dying or something," Brenda laughed at the sight of Lori rushing into the house. We sat on her bed and just had our last conversation. "Don't forget me," Brenda asked Lori. "Thank you so much."

Lori wrote about the experience to her Goddaughter Gina. *"We should have been driving around, having fun. We should have been shooting hoops or going out to eat pizza. It was very awkward to be sitting next to my best friend, a friend that would soon be dead. It didn't make sense. All of a sudden, it became crystal clear that we would never again be able to have a heart-to-heart talk. We would no longer see each other on this side of the grave."*

"Brenda asked me if there was a heaven. We had talked about it for months, but now she was knocking on heaven's door. She quietly asked me to prove to her that there was a heaven; that she wasn't dying in vain."

"I held her hand and cried, craving to show her Bible passages that assured heaven. However, that required a maturity and sophistication that was unavailable to me. So I simply sat with her, silent, hoping my presence helped her."

The horrible cancer that had attacked Brenda was about to claim her life. Brenda knew what was taking place and had questions for her mother. "She asked me, too, the day before, when am I going to die? When am I going to die? I told her I didn't know, no one knows. Only God knows when he wants to take you."

"She must have been ready then. She must have been hurting pretty bad when she said that."

Brenda had confided in her sister, Arlene, that she had terrible headaches. Doris found a note in her bedroom that she found a big lump on her breast.

Brenda tried to protect her mother until the final day. "Of course, she didn't tell me," Doris said. "The cancer from her leg had spread to her breast and then to her brain."

Dr. Travnicek or a nurse would come over to give Brenda morphine shots, trying to keep Brenda in as little of pain as possible. Finally, it was time for the final injection. Everyone said their goodbyes, knowing Brenda would not wake up from this final sleep.

To Lori, Brenda simply said, "I'll be seeing you." Both were scared of separation and happy the suffering was ending.

Lori wrote of the final hours to Gina. *"The big fear was that she'd freak out and basically gag herself to death as she tried to gasp for air. To prevent that, they wanted to drug her with some morphine. It was a bittersweet thing when that nurse walked into the Florian home and pulled out her little syringe; everyone knew it was for the best, but it was also the beginning of the end."*

"Her whole family was gathered around her. I was honored that they asked me to be there, in that most private of time."

"I held Brenda's hand a lot and I could not hold back the tears as I felt her hand get colder and colder. The nurse had predicted it, saying that her body was preserving energy and letting her limbs get less blood circulation."

"Brenda's breathing was very labored. She would slowly bring in air and we'd all silently count the seconds until she expelled it. Then we'd

silently count again until we heard her inhale once more."

Arlene recalled the last words from her younger sister after the morphine had been administered. "I remember her saying when she was in pain, "Why are you doing this?" And then she said, "Oh," and she laid back down. That was the last thing I remember."

Brian remembered his last words to his sister. "She asked me what she should do when she was ready to die," Brian said. "I said just go to sleep. About that time, her head just fell back."

Finally, the labored breathing stopped. "I remember that very last few breaths," Brian said. I don't know who was on the other side of Brenda. Trav did come over. He said, "I think our ordeal is over."

"After she passed away, I think all of us just sighed in relief. It took us not even one hour and that house was completely flipped back to what it used to be. We had a bed from the nursing home. We took that back. We got everything erased."

Lori wrote about her reaction when her best friend lost her fight to cancer. *"Everyone in the room was very sad yet I think we were all thankful that Brenda was no longer in pain."*

"I left then, and when I got into my car, the radio was playing a song that was very meaningful to me, by the group Chicago. The lyrics were about saying goodbye. I just sat there and cried."

"I went to find my mom; she was at the post office. I just went to her and she held me. I felt very strange. I knew Brenda's death was expected, but it was much bigger than I had prepared for. I wasn't sure what to do with my feelings."

When the Nets Came Down for Brenda

Chapter 29
<u>Brenda Remembered</u>

I was teaching my classroom when someone told me Lori Kreshel had been called out of school to be with Brenda. Jim Moore and I left as soon as school was out with the intention of one final visit. As we drove in the direction of the Florian house, we were skeptical of what we would find.

Jim and I knew Brenda's cancer was about to claim her life. As I pulled up to the curb outside the house, several family members were coming out of the house. Just one look on their faces told us we were too late. The porch Brenda loved to sit and visit with her friends would be empty of its very special occupant.

Brenda's funeral was set for Friday. It would be held in the auditorium at the high school. The funeral would be conducted exactly like Brenda had planned. It would be a beautiful event. Her goal would be achieved; everyone would cry their eyes out.

Friday was the day Dave Newmyer's sixth graders were to spend at Indian Cave Park in the far southeast corner of Nebraska. It marked the fifth year of the annual outdoor classroom camp-out.

My first year of teaching at Wilber-Clatonia had been as a sixth grade teacher. Paul Heller, the principal, and I had planned and ran the first outdoor classroom.

The next year, Dave was hired as the sixth grade teacher and I moved to junior high mathematics. He decided to keep the yearly event alive. As of this writing, the camp-out has gone on for 33 years. However, in 1984, there was no camp-out. Brenda's death affected the entire community. The annual event was cancelled.

Tim Cervny was in that sixth grade class. "Mr. Newmyer threatened us all year, if we were ornery, we weren't going to go on the camp-out," Tim said. "We understood, everyone understood; everyone was in touch with Brenda's death at that time. Even for sixth graders, we understood what was going on."

"I remember how Brenda's death impacted the adults," Tim said. "It was just weighing on everyone. I didn't go to the funeral. Before Brenda's death, I hadn't had any death experience. The whole community felt it."

A recent story in the Wilber Republican about Brenda brought back strong feelings for Tim. "I was quite a bit younger and I never knew her," Tim said. "I hadn't really thought of it for a long time until I read that article. I cried when I read it and I don't cry very often."

"I think that's because I'm a dad now. I understand how impactful it would be to lose somebody. Reading about how she handled things and how mature she was caused my reaction."

"We (his daughters) talked about Lori Kereshel. For those girls to be able to handle that, it was pretty amazing to me. I tried to help my kids to understand that life is precious. This girl went through a lot. There are still a lot of people around and this is someone's sister so they could internalize it."

Many tributes came to the Florian family after Brenda's death. A heart-felt, handwritten note came from Dr. Mark Hutchins, a Lincoln doctor who treated Brenda and helped with Brenda's wish to see Disney World. He wrote, *Thank you so much for trusting Brenda's care to me. She was a courageous person.*

I learned a lot about life from her. I will not forget her. I am happy for you and the family that she was able to remain at home. I know Dr. Trav cared for her deeply and did his best to help her in transition from living through dying. I will miss her.

Doris received a letter from someone Brenda had corresponded with since her amputation late in 1982. Governor Bob Kerry, who Brenda had drilled about his love life, wrote, *I write to you in this, your time of grief, to offer my condolences on Brenda's death.*

I realize that no words can take away the pain of the loss of a daughter, that no expression of sympathy can lessen the heartache that this time must bring. Please accept this only as my desire to let you know that another person shares your loss.

I was fortunate to have had the opportunity to meet with Brenda, to sense her strength, her courage, and her love. We must, in times like this, reflect on the life Brenda lived and attempt to find a measure of hope in the joy she brought to those who knew her.

Just as the world is diminished by her loss, so was it enriched by her life.

The Zajicek Funeral Home prepares a small information sheet that gives an obituary and the funeral schedule. Often a relevant poem included to help make sense of death. When I read the poem, I realized I knew the author. Ironically, it was written by a high school basketball player from Hebron.

I later called Kim Hissong for permission to put her poem in a trophy case display that honored Brenda next to the 1983 State Championship trophy. She had no idea the poem had been used at Brenda's funeral and she immediately gave her permission.

The poem read, *I saw God today, strolling through the meadow; Not quite sure of what He was doing. I decided to stay and watch, just a bit longer. I was impatient, my feelings were crushed. I wanted to scream, but instead I sat, Waiting quietly, with the curiosity of a child. Suddenly He turned and looked at me. I was startled, but quickly blurted out, "Why, God do some die so young? Why did you take my friend?" In all great wisdom, He replied, In much to my amazement with another question, "If you were gathering flowers, would you pick only the old for your bouquet?" Coming nearer, I felt His warmth. I touched His love. He opened His arms, into which I should climb, and said, "Come to Me, be My corsage." I think He was picking flowers.*

Another touching tribute came from the students of the 1985 graduating class. *Brenda was always very much a part of our lives. She had been known and loved by many, and all of us felt as if we had lost a part of ourselves along with her.*

Brenda's major interest—both in school and out—was people. She rarely would be seen outside a crowd and always seemed to know just how to cheer us when we were down.

Perhaps Brenda's strongest point was her ability to think of others before herself. Even before she died, she was more concerned about how her family and friends would handle her death than about herself.

Although we, the Class of 1985, feel a great deal of pain and sadness at the loss of our friend and companion, we also feel very lucky to have been given the chance to get to know and love her.

Despite all the tributes, Brenda's best friend would miss her the most. Shortly after her death, Lori went to the Zajicek Funeral Home for one last conversation with her constant companion. *No one was there,* Lori wrote in a letter. *I knelt down and had a talk with her. I kept thinking over and over. It was always just you and me. Now only I was left.*

Lori would soon prove to take the lessons learned over the past 18 months and use them to honor her friend. Lori's trails of adulthood were just beginning, but now she knew better than most how to handle life's problems.

Chapter 30
<u>Heaven and Butterflies</u>

Several years ago, one of my favorite television shows was Magnum P.I. starring Tom Selleck. I couldn't tell you the title of any of the separate episodes except one called Heaven and Jelly Donuts. Selleck gets the help he needs from a friend who had been killed in a car bomb meant for him. Magnum bribed the ghost with jelly donuts, a sure sign it was his friend.

When someone dies so young, friends and family look for answers that only come from faith. The mystery of life and death can't be factually solved. Once in a while, there is an occurrence that gives us hope that everything is fine.

My mother died when I was eight years old. My dad remarried 11 months later to a woman who had lost her husband about the same time my mother died. When I was older, Mae, my step-mother, told me a story about her first husband's death.

His name was Bill Greer and he suffered from ulcerated colitis. He often had flair-ups that caused him to enter the Veterans Hospital in Lincoln. During one of those stays in the hospital, Bill asked Mae to stay with him. He told Mae that the angels had visited him the night before and they were coming back to take him that night.

Mae wanted to stay, but the hospital policy was if a patient wasn't critical, relatives couldn't spend the night. It took Mae about 30 minutes to return to their home in southeast Lincoln. Just as she came in the front door, the phone was ringing. The hospital was calling to tell her Bill had passed away.

A few events surrounding Brenda and her death gave people hope that Brenda was indeed in peace and happy. Sunday night before her death on Monday, Brenda was sleeping on the hospital bed in the living room. Doris was sleeping close by on the couch.

Brenda woke her up with a strange story. "She told me the funniest thing happened," Doris said. "Brenda told me it felt like she was being lifted off my bed. I thought she was just imaging it, but she always told me the way it was."

Brian always had a special relationship with Brenda. After her death, he took out his anger by tearing around in his car. Later, Brian had a dream about Brenda.

"I dreamt that Jesus was carrying her down the street," Brian said. "Of course, he was tall. He was carrying Brenda and she said, "Look, here's my brother." It was a long time ago."

Lori Kreshel and her faith had provided tremendous support for Brenda during the 18 months of her illness. The entire Kreshel clan was a devoted Catholic family. Katie is a younger sister to Lori. Shortly after Brenda's death, Katie was down stairs in the family home. She had a strange vision.

"She said she was praying and all of a sudden, she saw Brenda," Lori said. "She saw Brenda, Jerome and Mary all standing there together. Brenda looked supremely happy and had a great, big smile on her face. She talked to Katie, but didn't move her mouth, "Tell Lori not to worry and that it will all work out." Then she said she was happy. Katie said aloud, "You want me to tell Lori." Then Brenda was gone."

The symbol of a butterfly is like a reminder of Brenda. Brenda loved butterflies. It was the butterfly that helped bring peace to one of her best friends.

Tim Bauman had a crush on Brenda when they attended school together. Although, they never dated, they became best friends. "We were like peas in a pod," Tim said. "We were close friends."

"I hoped someday I would find a girl like Brenda. After I was married, I took my wife (named Brenda, also) to introduce her to Doris. She said she even looked a little like Brenda. They had the same backgrounds, too."

Tim had met his wife while attending college at Northwest Missouri State University. Tim went into law enforcement and came back to work for the campus safety. He was good friends with the current head of campus safety, Clarence Green.

The couple tried to have children, but Brenda couldn't get pregnant. "It took several years," Tim said. "It was a miracle when it happened. The pregnancy went well."

As the birth of his son grew near, events began to complicate things. Tim had worked a long shift at the University. Brenda's water broke and she headed to the hospital in labor. Tim's grandmother had been seriously ill. He took his wife to the hospital, only to find out his mother wanted him home; his grandmother didn't have long to live.

The labor stretched into 18 hours. Tim's parents lived two hours from Maryville and Brenda's parents were an hour and a half from their daughter. Tim, who had been awake for over two days, was by himself as his wife continued to have difficulty in labor and a dying grandmother two hours away.

"The doctors told me I might have to leave," Tim said. "They were concerned about Brenda's health. Mom called me then and said Grandma won't live another 15 minutes. She wanted me to call and talk to her one last time."

"I had to walk out of the hospital for change to call Mom. I was stopped by a nurse to tell me my grandmother had died."

Burdened by worry for his wife and unborn son, saddened by the death of his grandmother, and way past exhaustion, Tim had all the events hit him at once. "At that moment, I thought, what would Brenda (Florian) think?" Tim said. "I'm looking up and there sitting on the hood of my truck was a butterfly. It was September and pretty cold. You wouldn't expect to see a butterfly."

The irony of thinking of his dead friend and the butterfly on his pickup did not escape Tim. He remembered Doris telling him about Brenda and the butterflies. When he started to walk back to the hospital, he was surrounded by what appeared to be over 100 butterflies.

"I cried my eyes out," Tim said. "That had to be Brenda telling me everything would be alright." Tim quickly entered the hospital to be with his wife. In the matter of minutes, a healthy boy was born.

Chapter 31
<u>The Exchange Student</u>

The story of Brenda's life ended on May 1, 1984. The story of Brenda's influence is still going on today. The family had each other for comfort. Lori had a large family, Brenda's family, and a host of friends to help her cope with the daily living without Brenda.

She also had a great adventure she had earned while dealing with Brenda's illness. There was a program called Youth for Understanding. Two juniors in high school would be picked from each state. The state senators would handle the selection. The 100 students would spend most of the summer in Japan with host families.

Lori had seen the advertisement as a sophomore. She wrote about the whole process and trip in a letter to Gina. " *I daydreamed, I knew I could be an exchange student if my parents were rich; anyone can travel. But this program was different. It was completely free.*"

A long process of filling out forms and getting people to write her references began for Lori. By now, she knew Brenda was dying from cancer. She was very reluctant to continue the application process. She didn't want to be on the opposite end of the earth when Brenda died. However, with Brenda's encouragement, she worked hard with the application processes.

As it turned out, Brenda was a major reason that Lori was still in the running. She wrote how her friend played another enormous role in her attempt to become an exchange student. *"I told the interviewers that Brenda told me that she would be much closer to me in Japan after she died than she was now, as we sat face to face. I didn't have any reservations about leaving."*

"When I told them that, I was very matter-of-fact, because that was the truth. I didn't think much about it. But you know, there were tons of applicants for that scholarship. I wish I could say I won the scholarship because of my talent, but I really think the fact that my best friend was dealing with life and death issues had some influence! I mean, I was not their typical applicant because of that. Of course, it was God's will."

"When I received word that I had won, I was ecstatic. My parents were so proud of me, Brenda was proud of me, I was proud of me. Brenda told me that after she died she would send me roses from heaven, like St. Therese of Lisieux, "The Little Flower."

In the middle of June, about six weeks after Brenda's death, Lori flew to Washington,

D.C. All 100 scholarship awardees would gather in the nation's capital for a week of orientation. On June 24, they would fly to Japan to begin the exchange program.

Lori loved the foreign culture and the unusual foods. Her host sister was named Ritsuko. Like Lori, she was a junior in high school. She lived with Ritsuko's family, which consisted of an adult sister who was in America and their parents in the city of Noda. Lori would come to love Ritsuko, but her experience in Japan was not what she expected.

She wrote, "*That summer was extremely difficult. Although my host parents were very kind, there was a huge barrier between us since they could not speak English. Ritsuko went to school every day. On some days I joined her and spent half the day with her in class and the other half in the library, or I stayed at their home.*"

"*I knew I was going to have a great summer, yet there seemed to be only challenges. In order to stay sane, I prayed the rosary constantly; most days I said the completed 15-decade rosary. I read the Bible. I journaled and prayed non-stop.*"

"*There would be times when I would be very depressed. Once I jogged over to a park and sat on the ground. I was completely barren emotionally. I needed strength. Then I saw a butterfly. It hovered all around me. As I stared at it, I became aware of other spiritual things. I felt the presence of God and Brenda right next to me. My soul was opened and it was filled. I left the park ready to handle the quiet."*

"Of the 100 exchange students, 98 had great experiences," Lori said. Unfortunately, Lori wasn't one of them. Not only was there silence from the language barrier, but the host family never took Lori sight-seeing nor did they travel the country of Japan.

Lori found out later that they hosted her so Ritsuko could learn English. The next year, Ritsuko would become an exchange student in the United States. They would save money for their daughter's trip by staying close to home. Lori would provide Ritsuko with the necessary English education so she could qualify for the foreign exchange program.

"The administrators from Youth for Understanding checked on me a lot, asking me if I was doing okay, if I needed another host family, or if I was happy where I was. I never considered leaving the Osaka Family. I loved them very much."

The family had a vacation planned to a tiny island to see a long-lost uncle. Lori looked forward to the vacation. It began poorly, however, when they all had to cram onto a little ship. Lori was forced to kick one of the travelers when his hands began to wonder too much.

"When we got there, the house we stayed at was a dump. Utterly and completely. The smell of the place was horrendous. The aunt and uncle were strange and demented. They made Ritsuko and I do all their chores. Flies were on everything, especially the food. Huge bugs crawled all over their house. In Japan people do not have beds. They sleep on the floor. We literally slept with the roaches. We were thrilled when that "vacation" was over!"

On July 19th, Brenda came to the rescue. Lori received a telegram from a surprising source. It read, *"Have a nice day, with love, Brenda."*

Lori wrote about her much-welcomed telegram from the United States. *"The telegram said I had an arrangement of red roses to pick up in Tokyo. What? A message from my dead friend? Well, it turns out Brenda and Doris had discussed it before she died and she told her mom she wanted to send me roses that summer while I was in Japan. I hugged the thought to my heart, Brenda sent me flowers!"*

By the time it was ready to come home to America, Lori understood the reason for her experiences in Japan. *"He (God) knew what I needed—quiet time. I was allowed time to think, pray and journal about my experience with Brenda. I was given the space and the quiet to simply be still, to be healed and to grow spiritually."*

Lori came home for her senior year at Wilber-Clatonia High School. She had one promise she had to keep. At Wilber-Clatonia Schools, it was a policy that the top 10 percent of the senior class speak at graduation. Brenda wanted Lori to give a speech for her.

Chapter 32
The Graduation Speech

Lori used the motivation Brenda provided to have a very successful high school athletic career. I left for Doane College before the 1984-1985 school year. Dave Grothen, my assistant coach, accepted the head coaching position. Jim Moore was his assistant coach.

The Wolverines played well, but were beaten badly twice by Centennial High School. Their young post players were now seniors and appeared poised for a state championship run. They faced each other for a third time in the district championship game at Crete High School.

I was in the crowd as Lori, Cheryl Wiese, Renee Wickwire and their teammates used a triangle and two defense to slow down the high-scoring Broncos. A late traveling call that an official almost missed led to the upset win. The official made the right call; it just came a few seconds late. Ironically, that official also worked our state championship game in 1983.

Despite playing excellent basketball, Wilber-Clatonia lost for the third consecutive year to Battle Creek in the state tournament. Lori had accomplished everything she promised

Brenda. The promise extended beyond athletics.

Brenda knew Lori would excel in academics, too. Through all four years of high school, Lori and Cheryl Wiese battled for valedictorian honors. In the end, Cheryl had beat out Lori by the narrowest of margins. However, both young ladies would give speeches at the 1985 graduation ceremonies.

I have listened to hundreds of graduation speeches over the years. I have heard motivational speakers, self-help speakers, evangelical ministers, thank-you speeches, acceptance speeches, graduation speeches, and speeches where people just like to talk.

There are three speeches that left an indelible mark on me. I was almost 11 years old when Mrs. Edna Hunt, my fifth grade teacher, forced me to listen to a speech. She marched all the kids in our classroom that consisted of third, four, and fifth graders to the Methodist minister's parsonage.

Ronnie Mindt was the minister's son and in the fifth grade. They had a black and white television in the parsonage. The school in Clatonia didn't have any of the new technology of 1961. Mrs. Hunt loved history and she wanted us all to watch John F. Kennedy's inauguration speech.

I was very sure I would be bored to death after the first two or three sentences. However, I couldn't take my eyes off the grainy screen. Toward the end, he said the most famous line from the speech. "Ask not, my fellow Americans," Kennedy proclaimed, "What your country can do for you – ask what you can do for your country."

The second speech that is locked in my memory is the prom speech about lost imagination. Some man claimed loss of imagination among America's youth at an alarming rate. For some reason, I believed every word he said and remembered forever.

Lori's graduation speech was the third unforgettable speech. "I knew I was going to be speaking because Cheryl Wiese beat me by 0.02 of a point," Lori said. "She was valedictorian."

"I knew who was top and I was working with Jim Dymacek. He said I needed to write a speech. I told Mr. Dymacek I was waiting for it to be written."

Jim Dymacek was the high school counselor during Lori and Brenda's high school days. Jim provided a supportive ear for Lori as she dealt with the pressures of her best friend dying.

"Brenda told me I needed to lead a good life," Lori said. "When I wrote the speech, I wrote it in one setting. It was totally inspired. Poor Jim said we needed to go through it all and I said I'm just waiting. It was like four days before graduation and I said okay. I was quiet and I just poured it on the paper."

After a brief introduction, Lori began her unforgettable speech. *"Today, I'd like to share with you a few things that have helped me in my life and which I hope will better each of your lives . . . not only the graduates, but everyone here."*

The middle third of Lori's speech talked of Brenda's unique courage. She told how Brenda was resigned to the fact she would never marry. As a substitute, she planned a grand funeral for herself.

If that didn't grab the audience's attention, the final third of the speech felt like it was coming right out of Brenda's mouth. *"I see so many people spending all of their energy worrying over trivial matters, such as their hair, their boyfriend/girlfriend, money and job situation . . . if they'd only realize what life is really about. I guess that's my main point for you today."*

"Having someone close to you die, suddenly puts everything in prospective. I believe you learn about life through death. You really learn what's important and what's not in this world."

"The big challenge is to take today and live it to the very limit. Bring joy to those around you. Be spontaneous!"

"If you always yearned to give someone flowers, do it today. Don't wait until an accident occurs and you end up having to decorate their casket with them."

If you love something or someone, tell them, make them happy, while they are still with you. Don't ever let any opportunities pass you by."

"I'd like to finish by telling you something Brenda told me, before she died. She went, "Lori, I want you to take your life and live it to its full potential. Don't settle for less. It's so exciting that you are alive and can do anything you desire."

"She said she'd be in heaven, waiting for us all, but, well, she didn't really know about heaven, because she had never been there. Although she knew she'd go there soon, at the time, heaven was into the unknown. All she knew then, before she died, was that people she was leaving behind were ALIVE! She was so happy for them and she hoped everyone learned to love and enjoy life, because they didn't know how lucky there were, JUST TO BE ALIVE."

Since that was my friend's farewell message to me, I decided to make it my farewell message *to you. I only hope it enriches your life as much as it has enriched mine."*

Brenda was buried on Friday, May 5, 1984. She told Lori she hoped everyone cried their eyes out. Brenda accomplished that one more time in the spring of 1985. There wasn't a dry eye in the crowd, except for the speaker.

Acknowledgements

I made up my mind in the fall of 2011 that I would write a book about Brenda Florian. I was absolutely sure that people would laugh at the thought of a basketball coach trying to enter the literary world. I was surprised that most people were supportive.

It all started at the fence that separates the property of the Ginger Bread House, owned by Arlene (Florian) Albert and Dave and Janet Newmyer, friends of mine during my days of teaching at Wilber-Clatonia School. Doris Florian was helping her daughter with the day care. She met me at that fence and I asked her if she would give me permission to write the book.

Doris tearfully agreed, but I had to wait a couple of weeks while Bob Maly, a widower and Doris's husband, took a trip through the Panama Canal. While I awaited their return, my first interview was with a friend and former assistant coach, Dave Grothen. The ball was now rolling.

On a football Saturday afternoon, the entire Florian family gathered at Doris and Bob's house. We talked, laughed and cried for several hours. I knew when I walked out of that house I had a special topic. Now my job was not to screw it up.

Doris and her children Alan, Brian, Arlene, and Melissa have been terrific with their time. They have been patient with me as I interrupted their lives with questions about a very painful past.

Soon after that Saturday afternoon, I visited Lori (Kreshel) Doorman near Wichita, Kansas, where she lives with her husband and children. It was a rainy afternoon and it was a very powerful three hours as we talked about her dear friend. The four-hour drive home gave me the quiet time to organize my thoughts and emotions.

My most sincere thanks go out to everyone that contributed. Many of the state championship team members responded to my request for information. Her friends told amazing stories and were very generous to me. The teachers who I called were terrific, especially Dave Grothen, Jim Moore, Lori Connot, and Dennis Potthoff.

After almost 30 years, I hope my timing of events is accurate. My only hope is I don't disappoint the Florian family with my lack of writing talent. The tale of Brenda Florian and the legacy she left deserves much more talent than I could offer.

<u>Where are They Now?</u>

The Florian family has flourished in the years since Brenda's death in 1984.

As the summer of 2012 approaches, Doris' oldest child, Alan, lives in Loveland, CO with his wife, Kim. They have two grown children, Kylie and Justin. He owns a construction company.

Brenda's older sister, Arlene, who took Brenda on a final jog in Rochester, MN, lives in Wilber with her husband, Scott Albert. She owns and operates the Gingerbread Day Care. They have three children; Gina (who lives in Wichita, KS, close to her God Mother, Lori), Barry and Stephanie.

Brian, the older brother who taught Brenda to drive with one leg, also lives in Wilber. He owns the Wilber Body Shop. Brian is married to Judy. Brenda matched Judy to Brian at the Sokol Hall dance. They have three children, Natasha, Brad, and Marissa.

Melissa, Brenda's younger sister who was lovingly nicknamed, Pissy Missy, lives in Lincoln, NE. She is married to Todd Blome. Melissa is a nurse. They have three school-age children, Megan, Michael, and Matthew.

Doris remarried widower, Bob Maly, sixteen years ago. She is retired and living in a house on the west end of Wilber. Ironically, Bob was on the Wilber-Clatonia School Board during my five years of employment at the school.

The refrigerator sits in the kitchen and is not discussed like the bathroom refrigerator in the old house by the Elementary School. Beside the 11 grandchildren, Doris is a great-grandmother to two others.

Doris visits Brenda's grave with flowers every birthday and most holidays. She had her picture put on a heart-shaped tombstone. No one will ever forget her daughter.

Lori (Kreshel) Doerneman lives near Wichita, KS, with her husband, Russ and her eight children.

Russ is an engineer for Lear Jet and Lori, a former teacher, is a stay-home mom. She calls it, "raising her own basketball team." Their children range in age from 19 to 3.

From oldest to youngest, Lori's team includes Eric, Rachel, Mitchell, Matthew, Malaysia, Bridget, Thomas, and David.

The intense relationship with Brenda as a teenager is a permanent influence on Lori. "The experience remains close to my heart and continues to influence my choices, especially how I relate with people," Lori said.